EVERYDAY THEOLOGY FOR CATHOLIC ADULTS

DARYL OLSZEWSKI

Everyday Theology
for Catholic Adults

the columba press

This edition, 1991, published by
THE COLUMBA PRESS
93 The Rise, Mount Merrion, Blackrock, Co Dublin, Ireland

First published in the United States of America by
Hi-Time Publishing Corp., Milwaukee, Wisconsin.

Cover by Bill Bolger
Origination by The Columba Press
Printed in Ireland by Genprint, Ltd., Dublin.

ISBN 1 85607 018 2

Nihil Obstst:
Reverend Monsignor John F Murphy
Censor Librorum
September 2nd 1989

Imprimatur:
✠ Most Reverend Rembert G Weakland OSB
Archbishop of Milwaukee
September 2nd 1989

Contents

To my best friend, lover, wife,
Betty,
with all my love.

Foreword

Daryl Olszewski has put together a book that has long needed to be written. It confronts those issues and questions that have been on the minds and lips of Catholics since the closing session of the Second Vatican Council.

The Second Vatican Council was a magnificent, much-needed, Spirit-filled event in the history of the Roman Catholic Church. The documents produced by the council fathers gave the Church new theological insights, refined old ones, and prepared our theology for the twenty-first century. All those who read the documents grew in their faith and in their understanding of the Church. However, the process for the implementation of the council directives was too hastily mandated and too superficially understood to have the desired impact on the person in the pew or the priest at the altar. Daryl Olszewski's new book, *Everyday Theology for Catholic Adults*, will be a marvellous addition to the library of any Catholic because the insights he generates will help the development of a solid and updated understanding of the Church.

I see this little volume as a welcome tool in the resource kit of parish catechists. Our young people, as we know, are more and more a questioning people, and this book will assist catechists in formulating solid responses to their queries. All of us in the teaching ministry of the Church have at times been guilty of giving slipshod answers. With *Everyday Theology for Catholic Adults* in our hands, that need not happen.

I envision this book on the coffee tables and reading tables of searching Catholics and potential Catholics everywhere. Isn't it true that Catholics love to talk about their faith, their parish, their priest, their bishop? This book will help them 'get a handle' on some of the most frequently talked-about issues today. It will answer their questions, thereby enabling them to move on to a deeper understanding of their faith.

And finally, for the practicality and originality of Mr Olszewski's insights, I envision this book on the desks of parish priests everywhere. I can see this volume being the basis of adult education programmes the country over.

It is recorded in these pages that, through the Second Vatican Council, Pope John 'allowed the Church to have a good "spring-cleaning".' After a spring-cleaning a home may look different. 'The furniture might be rearranged and the walls might be a different colour, but it is still home.' So it is with the Church after the Second Vatican Council. *Everyday Theology for Catholic Adults* will help us appreciate this home even more.

Reverend Leonard M. Barbian
Pastor
St Mary Faith Community
Hales Corners, Wisconsin.

Introduction

Dear Reader,

Thanks for opening this book. Please allow me to tell you a little about it before you turn to the next section.

In the early 1970s the late Fr Melvin Farrell wrote a series of articles for Hi-Time magazine, which were intended 'to help teachers and parents understand current theological thinking' immediately after the Second Vatican Council. These articles were eventually published in the popular book, *Theology for Parents and Teachers*. When Hi-Time asked me to update Fr Farrell's book, I found that the rephrasing of a few paragraphs and the mere changing of a quotation, name or date, were inadequate for addressing the types of questions people seemed to be asking about the Catholic faith today. Thus, this present book was undertaken.

This book is *not intended* to provide comprehensive answers to *all* of the questions Catholics are asking today. Rather, it is intended to highlight some of the more common questions. I can only hope that I have provided answers as insightfully and succinctly as Fr Farrell did previously.

The classic definition of theology is 'faith seeking understanding'. The title, *Everyday Theology for Catholic Adults*, implies a popular or simplified theology. In other words, this book is written for the 'average' Catholic, the questioning Catholic who simply wants to understand the faith a little better. If you have questions about the Catholic faith, if you are seeking answers to what the Church teaches and how it lives and celebrates its faith, if you want to understand what your children or your grandchildren are being taught, then it is my hope that you have come to the right place.

I would like to express my deep appreciation to Michael Vogl of Hi-Time for his confidence and support in giving me the opportunity to work in this dimension of the Ministry of the Word. Special thanks to the editors, Lorraine Kukulski, Karen Cannizzo and Sr

Alice Ann Pfeifer,C.S.A., for their patience and understanding and for their expertise in taking the raw manuscript and turning it into a beautiful finished product. They are special people, and I thank them for their hard work and loving friendship.

I am also grateful to Monsignor John F. Murphy and to Fr Alfred McBride, O.Praem., for their careful reading of the manuscript and for their valuable suggestions.

Special thanks to Fr Leonard Barbian for his insights, support and encouragement, and for his kind words of introduction for this book.

I am indebted to many adults, especially those at St Matthias, Mary Queen of Heaven, and St Mary's, who raised the types of questions found in this book.

The gift of faith was first expressed to me through the deep love and faith of my parents, John and Dolores, and for them I give great thanks to the Lord. That faith continues to be nurtured and sustained in sacramental love; and so, to my beautiful wife, Betty, who gave me the time to write this book, I express my deep love and appreciation. Also, many thanks to our children, Rebecca and D.J., who were very understanding as they patiently waited for Dad to complete this project.

Finally, thanks to you, the reader, for taking the time to share in this quest for greater understanding of our faith. May this experience lead to a deeper knowledge of God, which, in turn, leads to greater love and unselfish service for the sake of the kingdom.

Daryl Olszewski
May 31, 1989,
Feast of the Visitation

CHAPTER 1

Why the changes in the Church?

Why are there changes in the Catholic Church? Why can't things just remain the same or be as they were in the 'good ol' days'?

Some people see change as a sign of growth, a sign that the Catholic Church is moving forward, catching up with the times. Others are disturbed by change. They see change as a sign of deterioration, a sign that we, as Church and as individual Catholics, are losing sight of who we are and what it really means to be Catholic.

In addressing the question of changes in the Church, it is important to understand what can change and what can never change. The Church is the Body of Christ, the visible presence of the resurrected Christ in the world. To know Christ is to know what the Church should be. The Church is Christ. That can never change. As Jesus said, '... behold, I am with you always, until the end of the age' (Mt 28:20).

The purpose of the Church, its ultimate mission, is the same as Christ's – to bring about the kingdom of God, to proclaim the Good News of salvation to all people and, ultimately, to bring all people to the fullness of life with God.

To understand what can change and what cannot change in the Church, it might be helpful to compare the Church to a human person. I am a human being, composed of body and soul. That is my nature or what I essentially am. As a human being, I have an ultimate purpose, to be the best person I can be, which means that, in time, I want to share in the love of God totally. My nature cannot change, but I can freely choose either to fulfill or not to fulfill my ultimate purpose. My thoughts and actions can change. My physical form can change and is changing at this very moment. But my nature cannot change.

As I look back on my life, I know that I am the same person I have always been, but I also know that I have changed in the way I think and act. I have come to know myself better and to know the kind of person I should be. I have experienced internal changes, which have led to different ways of acting. I have come to understand my nature better, but my basic nature hasn't changed.

Throughout my life I have experienced different roles – child, student, husband, employee, father. Each has caused me to act in a certain way. But underneath all these roles, I'm still the same me.

We might find it helpful to look at the Church in this way. Its identity or nature has always been the same. Its ultimate purpose has always been the same. But the Church's expression of its identity and purpose has changed over the years. We would not expect a forty-year-old person to behave as she or he did at twenty years of age or ten years of age. So imagine the behavioural changes that would take place if a person lived two thousand years!

The Church has grown and changed just as any person would grow and change in two thousand years. But it is still the same 'person'. The Church itself is constantly experiencing conversion, seeing its ultimate purpose in new ways, and coming to a deeper realisation of what that purpose is. But the Church's nature doesn't change. The Church remains the Church.

Just as all people experience in their lives a variety of roles that cause them to act in a variety of ways, so does the Church. In its infancy the Church was a persecuted, outlawed group that had to hide and protect itself in order to survive. This persecution caused the Church to act in certain ways, but it never changed the Church's nature, its identity.

At one point in history, the Church was given status equal to that of kings and rulers. After becoming a landlord and a temporal ruler, the Church began to act in certain ways. But underneath these developments, it was still the same Church.

The Church was, at one time, threatened with division, almost as if its limbs had been torn from its body. That would certainly cause anyone to act in a defensive way, and the Church did. But it was still the same Church.

The Church has sought to reconcile its quarrelling factions, to heal its divisions, and to serve as a voice for the poor and oppressed.

These actions may be different from actions the Church has pursued in the past, but the Church is still the same Church.

The Church is a living organism. It grows and changes. It experiences the death and regeneration of its cells. While a person may become wrinkled and grey-haired, the person's identity remains the same. The Church, too, changes, but it remains the Body of Christ.

Changes in the human body, just like changes in the Church, do not always come easily. Often, there is pain and even rebellion. Look at what happens when a person goes on a diet or begins a programme of rigorous exercise. Some parts of the body react better than others do, almost seeming to breathe a sigh of relief. Yet, some muscles ache and rebel painfully. Even during this time of change, however, the nature and purpose of the body remain the same.

Just as some parts of a person's body may not be ready for a change in the person's routine, so some members of the Church may be unprepared for a change in Church practice. Often, with change, there is pain. Sometimes there is rebellion. Some people cling to the past and refuse to change, while others, eager for change, race ahead.

Change is nothing new to the Church. One of the earliest examples of change came only some fifteen years after Pentecost. One group in the Church clung to the belief that Christians had to remain faithful to all the Mosaic laws, including the law requiring circumcision of males and the laws regulating diet. Another group claimed that obeying these laws was not necessary.

The showdown for dealing with this issue came at the Council of Jerusalem. The story is recorded in the fifteenth chapter of the Acts of the Apostles. Which side won? Well, we know, for example, that males today do not have to be circumcised in order to become Catholic, that Catholics are not prohibited from eating pork, and that they do not need to keep separate cooking utensils for certain kinds of food. But we can imagine that not everyone was happy with the decisions of this Council. There could well have been some Christians who continued to follow strictly the Mosaic laws, at least for a while.

Change takes time. It doesn't happen overnight. A person doesn't lose fifty pounds in one day. Not every muscle becomes firm with one workout. Change comes slowly and is not always permanent.

History seems to have a way of repeating itself, even in the Catholic Church.

Here are just a few examples:
- In the early Church, Masses were celebrated in the vernacular, not only in Latin.
- For about the first three hundred years most Masses were celebrated in homes rather than in churches.
- Lyres and harps, not organs, were often used to accompany the singing.
- Eucharist was received under both species, bread and wine.
- Priests in the Western Rite of the Catholic Church were once permitted to be married.
- Bishops were elected by the people.
- The RCIA was used for about the first five hundred years in the Church.

The list could go on and on. At any point in the history of the Church there have been changes, and probably pain and agony were involved. Each generation has probably asked, 'Why are they changing the Church? We like it just as it was!' The Church changes because it is a living organism. It responds to its own 'aging' process. It takes on different roles in history. It responds to its environment just as any living organism does.

The essentials of the Church, its nature and its purpose, have never changed. Its central dogmas, statements of what it is and what it believes, haven't changed and will not change. But each generation finds new ways to live out the Church's mission and comes to new understandings of the Church's nature and purpose. The Church wouldn't be alive if it didn't change. Thank God it does!

CHAPTER 2

What was Vatican II?

How quickly time flies! While many Catholics can vividly remember the Second Vatican Council, or Vatican II, and the tremendous changes that occurred in the Church because of it, there is a whole new generation of Catholics born after Vatican II who wonder what this event was. What was Vatican II? What changed in the Church? What are the documents of Vatican II?

When Pope John XXIII was elected pope in 1958, he was an old man who some cardinals thought would be a good caretaker of the Church but little else. However, Pope John had no intention of just sitting back and waiting to die. Within a few months of his election, Pope John called for the convening of the twenty-first ecumenical council in the history of the Church. It was to be held at the Vatican, where only one other council had ever been held, and that had been in 1869. Thus, this council was known as the Second Vatican Council, or Vatican II.

A council is a gathering of the bishops that is called by the pope. Ecumenical means worldwide. In all, some 2600 bishops from all over the world participated in Vatican II, the largest number of bishops ever to participate in a council.

Generally, councils are called to deal with some doctrinal matter, usually to combat a heresy or to clarify a doctrine that is being misinterpreted. But there wasn't any immediate doctrinal issue affecting the Church in 1958, so what was the point of calling a council? Pope John best described his reason when he symbolically opened the windows of the Vatican. It was like saying, `Let some fresh air in!'

In the 1500s the Church had closed its doors and windows in an effort to protect itself from the effects of the Protestant revolt. The Catholic Church became highly organised and legalistic. Organisation and legalism are not necessarily bad, but when they stifle creativity, research, openness and advancement of thought, they hinder growth. The Church became introspective and defensive in order to protect itself. But one can remain locked up for only so long.

Even before Vatican II, there had been stirrings in theological and catechetical circles, hints that changes were about to occur. Pope Leo XIII had moved the Catholic Church into the arena of worldly affairs with his letter on labour, *Rerum Novarum*. Pope Pius X had lowered the age for the reception of First Communion to the 'age of reason.' And Pope Pius XII had encouraged biblical scholarship. Vatican II simply seemed to be the event that allowed much pent-up energy and enthusiasm to explode.

Much work went into preparing for the council, and not until 1962 was it finally convened. Vatican II lasted three years and produced sixteen documents, which are often quoted in Catholic theology. The list of these documents shows the scope of concerns Vatican II dealt with:

- The Constitution on the Sacred Liturgy
- Decree on the Means of Social Communication
- Dogmatic Constitution on the Church
- Decree on the Catholic Eastern Churches
- Decree on Ecumenism
- Decree on the Pastoral Office of Bishops in the Church
- Decree on the Up-to-date Renewal of Religious Life
- Decree on the Training of Priests
- Declaration on Christian Education
- Declaration on the Relation of the Church to Non-Christian Religions
- Dogmatic Constitution on Divine Revelation
- Decree on the Apostolate of Lay People
- Declaration on Religious Liberty
- Decree on the Church's Missionary Activity
- Decree on the Ministry and Life of Priests
- Pastoral Constitution on the Church in the Modern World

Just by looking at these titles we can see that virtually no aspect of Catholic life was left unaddressed by the bishops. The bishops' statements were not just pious reflections or meditations. Rather, they were bold proclamations that mandated changes or at least set a course of action for developing future changes.

It is probably still too early to judge the historical significance of Vatican II. But, if nothing else, Vatican II should be recognised for the important role it played in moving the Church from introversion to extroversion – that is, from excessive concern about its internal rules and regulations to a renewed concern about its mission to the world. Catholic, after all, means universal. As a result of Vatican II, the Catholic Church has challenged and even empowered itself to be actively involved in the world and to transform the world according to the message of Christ.

The average Catholic found the most noticeable changes from Vatican II in the celebration of the sacraments, especially the Eucharist. Before Vatican II the Mass was a private matter; the priest 'said' Mass while the people prayed quietly. The Mass was conducted in Latin, a language few Catholics understood. Many Catholics therefore followed along by praying from a missal or prayer book. The altar was against the back wall of the church, and so the priest said Mass with his back to the people. Mass was something to watch and listen to, but not really to participate in. The way we celebrate Mass today is much different from what it was in the early 1960s.

There were many other external changes, including the way priests and religious sisters dressed and the way church buildings were designed. Strict laws regarding fasting and abstinence were relaxed. A trademark of Catholics before Vatican II was their practice of not eating meat on Fridays.

But perhaps more important than these changes were the changes of attitude that the Church had about itself and others. The Church before Vatican II generally meant the pope, bishops, and priests. While the Church was defined as the Mystical Body of Christ with Christ as the head, the visible head was the pope. Vatican II changed the emphasis from a hierarchical Church to a collegial Church, one in which the bishops work more closely with the pope and in which all people are united in the workings of the Church. Thus, Vatican II gave great impetus to the emergence of the role that the laity has in the Church today. This means that not only the pope, bishops and priests are to be actively involved, but all baptised people are to witness Christ in the world.

Another result of Vatican II was a change in the Catholic Church's attitude toward other religions. The Catholic Church, while not compromising its basic doctrine of being the one true Church of Christ, has seen that there is salvation outside of the Catholic Church, since it is God who saves. However, the Church eventually hopes to bring all people together into one fold.

Finally, Vatican II brought a change that has quietly affected Catholic thought, made profound changes in it, and yet is difficult to label. It is a theological change in emphasis in which God is seen less as being 'out there' and more as being 'with us'. This change in emphasis has affected our understanding of the sacraments, especially Eucharist and Penance; affected our piety and devotions; and, in general, revolutionised our moral lives. God is no longer someone to be feared but someone who loves us. God has come among us and continues to care for us no matter how much we sin.

The changes brought about by Vatican II came too quickly for some people, not allowing them enough time to adjust. These people are likely to feel that the changes brought about by Vatican II were too far-reaching. But others feel that Vatican II did not do enough. These people feel that the Council dragged its feet and avoided the major reforms that are needed. Actually, the Church is still reflecting on the Second Vatican Council and its place in the life of the Church today.

What Vatican II documents should the average Catholic read today? If I were to recommend one, I would recommend the one that I think will stand for many years as the hallmark document of Vatican II. That is the *Dogmatic Constitution on the Church*, or *Lumen Gentium* ('Light of all Nations'). This document provides a challenging view of the Church, and we have scratched only the surface of its meaning since Vatican II.

Pope John opened the window and let in some fresh air. He allowed the Church to have a good 'spring-cleaning'. But home is still home after we spring-clean. It may look different, brighter, and cleaner. The furniture might be rearranged and the walls might be a different colour, but it is still home.

So it is with the Church after Vatican II – the Church is still the Church.

CHAPTER 3

Religious Education – does it ever end?

We never stop learning. No matter who we are or how old we are, we can always learn something new. Modern technology forces us to learn new ways of doing things, from banking with a computer teller, to operating a new appliance, to filling in an income tax form. From scientific advances, we can learn how to grow the perfect tomato and the most beautiful rose or how to live healthier lives. Long after we complete our formal schooling, we still continue to learn. But what about our religion? When does our religious education end?

Many Catholics consider their religious education finished when they leave school – as if they have learned everything there is to know about their faith by the age of sixteen or even eighteen. Why, when people continue to learn so many new things in life, do so many of them stop learning about their faith?

One reason may be a misunderstanding of what religion is and, therefore, what the content of religious education is. Religion is the expression of our relationship with God. Many people view religion as simply being knowledge *about* God. For them, religion and religious education become merely a set of doctrines or beliefs to be known or memorised. Religious education becomes the means by which they learn things; for example, the Ten Commandments, the Trinity, the seven sacraments, the mysteries of the rosary. Many people think that once they know these things, once they have the 'answers', their religious education stops.

Religion is about a relationship between God and us. Healthy relationships continue to grow and develop. In a healthy relationship, we never stop learning about the other person, and we always learn more about ourselves from that person.

One implication of the word *education* is the idea of nourishment. If we view education as nourishment for our lives, then we can see it as a life-giving force rather than as a process by which we memorise and learn facts. Religious education then can be seen as nourishment for our relationship with God. We would never want to be undernourished, and we never outgrow our need to be nourished. Thus, religious education never ends. It is for all people and all ages. A number of years ago, in a document entitled *To Teach as Jesus Did*, the bishops of the United States defined three dimensions of catechetics or religious education. These are *message, community* and *service* (paragraph 14). To these a fourth dimension could be added as part of what the Christian community should do, namely *worship*. These four dimensions comprise the total educational mission of the Church and should be seen as a totality, with each part being equally important.

The *message* dimension includes the revelation of God through the Scriptures and Church tradition – in short, our doctrines and beliefs. This dimension has often received the greatest attention and sometimes the only attention in religious education. But the message does not stand alone. It is incomplete by itself. The message is about God's love, expressed in its fullness through Jesus Christ, continued in the Church (*community*), which continues the mission of Christ (*service*), and which brings people together to pray and celebrate (*worship*).

The Church is a *community* of believers in Jesus Christ. Religion is not simply something personal between God and me, but between God and *us*. As a community, we act together, pray together and are faithful to the message together. Saint Paul described this community of the Church as a body in which each person is a part, and each person is important, and in which we together make up the body of Christ (1 Corinthians 12:12-31).

Thus, religious education strives to build up that body and calls for us not only to 'know things', but also to live in the spirit of fellowship about which Jesus said, 'This is how all will know that you are my disciples, if you have love for one another' (John 13:35). The community dimension looks to the message for understanding and together they result in *service* and *worship*.

The *service* dimension involves the practical living of the Gospel. It means learning how to apply the Gospel to daily life, individually and communally. The message of the Gospel is not, 'Believe, go to church on Sundays and be saved... The message of the Gospel calls us to service, which is best described in John's account of the Last Supper at which Jesus washed the feet of his disciples. Washing feet was a lowly task relegated to slaves and servants. Yet Jesus, the Master, washed his disciples' feet and then offered this reason: '... so that as I have done for you, you should also do' (John 13:15). Thus, one of the purposes of religious education should be to teach us how to 'wash feet', that is, how to be of service.

In attempting to teach service through projects that help others, many religious education programmes begin with the youngest child. Many Confirmation programmes require teenage participants to complete service projects. The adult faith community also needs to learn continually how to 'wash feet', so that members can be of service to one another and to those beyond the faith community. Ultimately, service has to be a free and loving response to God, not just a class project or homework assignment. Service flows from what we know through the message, through our love for others in community, and through our prayerful relationship with God.

Although the *worship* dimension is the last considered here, it is not the least important, because all four dimensions are of equal importance. We *worship* God because of what we know (*message*), because of who we are (*community*), and because of the great works God does through us (*service*). When we worship, we also come to know God better (*message*) as a group of believers (*community*), and we are strengthened for our mission (*service*). Thus, these four dimensions of religious education flow from and lead to each other in a continuous circle.

These four dimensions are not really new in the Church. In the Acts of the Apostles we read: 'They devoted themselves to the teaching of the apostles and to the communal life, to the breaking of the bread and to the prayers. Awe came upon everyone, and many wonders and signs were done through the apostles' (Acts 2:42-43). Thus, from the earliest times in the Church, *message, community, service* and *worship* were woven together as part of Christian formation or religious education.

These four dimensions of religious education should be included in the total religious education of all people, regardless of age. However, depending upon the age-group involved, religious education will take on different forms. The education of young children should certainly be different from the education of older youth. The religious education of adults should involve a variety of methods appropriate to adult learning.

But who is responsible for carrying out this gigantic task of providing religious education for people of all ages? Simply, it is the Church. But the Church is not a group 'out there'; it is not only the bishops and priests. We are the Church, you and I. So all of us are responsible for carrying out this teaching mission.

Parents have a special role in this teaching mission because they are the first teachers of their children. Through the words and example of parents, children learn about the message, they learn how to worship, they learn how to be of service, and they experience their first community in the family setting. As children grow, parents may be asked to be involved in the formal religious education of the children, especially at times of sacramental preparation. These are opportunities not only for parents to be intimately involved in handing on the faith to their children, but also for them to learn more about their faith at an adult level.

Some people have the special gift of being catechists or religion teachers. Using this gift is an important way to live out the service dimension of religious education and to show others what it means to be of service. Children in a classroom or youth on a retreat probably learn more from what the teacher or group leader does than from what that person says. The personal witness of the catechist is one of the most important influences in shaping the faith of students.

But all Catholics, no matter what they do or who they are, teach others about the meaning of the Catholic faith by the way in which they live it. At work, in the community, at home, in our socialisation and recreation, others can see by what we say and do that our religion is not just a 'thing', but a lived faith that expresses our relationship with God.

The result of religious education is that our lives are different. Religious education results in a change, a conversion, over and over again. It attempts to accomplish what the Baltimore Catechism gave as an answer to why God made us. God made us to know (*message*), love (*worship*) and serve (*service*) him. We do this as a *community* of believers in the Catholic Church.

For some people, what is contained in the rest of this book may be a review (which never hurts); and for others, some information and concepts may be new. Whatever the case may be, it is hoped that all this will contribute to continuing our religious education so that our faith is not only in our heads but also in our hearts, for we never stop learning and loving.

CHAPTER 4

Church teaching – where does conscience fit in?

My father used to say, 'So long as you live in this house, you obey the rules of this house.' There wasn't much room for discussion and certainly no room for dissent from his statement. Although my father wasn't as unreasonable and inflexible as his statement may have made him seem, he was saying that there were certain rules that formed the essence of belonging to the Olszewski family. These could almost be called our family core doctrines. There was no room for disagreeing with them unless a family member wanted to move down the road and live with the Smith family.

A similar reality exists in the Catholic Church. There are certain core doctrines that form the Roman Catholic faith. To dissent from these beliefs removes a person from this religious family. 'So long as you live in this house, you obey the rules of this house' may just as well be said of our life in the Church.

The core of our Catholic beliefs has been revealed to us in the person of Jesus Christ, through the Scriptures, and through our tradition. The doctrines or teachings that carry the greatest weight are called *dogmas*. Believing these teachings is absolutely essential to being a Catholic Christian. Examples of dogmas are belief in the oneness of God, the incarnation, the resurrection of Christ, and the Trinity.

A *doctrine*, too, is official Church teaching, but total acceptance of a particular doctrine is not always seen as essential to one's remaining a member of the Catholic Church.

The teaching authority of the Church resides with the pope and the bishops; however, others also share in various ways in the gift of teaching. When the Church teaches, it is assumed that prayerful consideration has been given to any official statement and that those who are competent in the field have been consulted on the matter. Thus, for instance, when the pope issues an encyclical or papal letter, this teaching is to be taken seriously.

Any disagreement with papal teachings requires a prayerful, serious and studious examination of the teaching. The technical knowledge required is often more than the average individual has. Why is it, then, that many people seem to find it easy to disagree with certain Church teachings? The mass media have enabled us to be more readily informed about Church teachings. But at the same time, the media have often contributed to confusion in the Church. Sometimes even before a document is published by the Church, opposing viewpoints are being heard. Our communication is instantaneous, and the media can certainly influence the way a teaching might be perceived by the public. It is unfortunate that many Catholics rely solely upon the evening news or secular press as their source of information about Catholic teachings.

It is also unfortunate that theologians and bishops, who have a right and duty to examine Church teachings and to further clarify them when necessary, sometimes use public forums for their debates. In many instances this only serves to confuse the majority of people, lay and ordained, who are not fully informed about the issues.

But while the media can mislead and confuse, they can at least be given credit for notifying the majority of people that Church teachings exist. Catholics today, especially in modern countries, have almost no excuse for not being informed about current Church teachings.

Perhaps the most modern example of a controversial Church teaching came from Pope Paul VI's encyclical, *Humanae Vitae*. The total document was actually a beautiful statement on the sacredness of life and marriage. Unfortunately, what was highlighted was the prohibition against any form of artificial contraception. An important question for many Catholics is, 'Can a person in some way dissent from this teaching and still remain a Roman Catholic Christian?' Even if a Catholic, according to his or her conscience, says 'Yes', it remains important to consider how a person arrives at such dissent, not only with this document but with any Church teaching.

A person cannot easily disagree with Church teaching. A person cannot base a decision solely on feelings or the belief that 'everyone else is doing it'. The important matter of conscience formation must

be considered. What does it mean to have a well-formed conscience?

Conscience is the ability to decide ultimately what must be done in
a given situation. We do not arrive at this ability easily. To have a
well-formed conscience, we should become fully informed about
an issue. Thus, in the case of Church teaching, we should read the
document concerned with the issue, and become aware of the document's contents through careful attention to the preaching and
teaching of homilists and theologians.

A well-formed conscience would also be attuned to the Scriptures
and previous Church teachings on the issue. This often requires
serious study and thus points out the need for continuing religious
education for adults. At the very least, a person should consult
with a spiritual advisor, pastor or other similarly qualified person
about the issue.

It is also important to develop a vital spiritual life that includes
prayer, participation in the sacraments, and living the Gospel daily.
Thus, a person is able to consider an issue by prayerfully asking
how this decision fits into the total picture of his or her Christian
life.

When a person finally arrives at a decision, he or she must act upon it
in order to be true to the self. Sometimes this requires great courage,
but a person cannot violate his or her conscience. This does not
mean, however, that a person cannot change a stand after careful
and prayerful reconsideration.

Unfortunately, many people take their consciences too lightly and
do not give the full and serious consideration that is due to an issue
or moral act. Sometimes people read an article or hear a priest or
lay person say something in an adult education class, and they
readily accept this statement because it happens to suit their needs.
Paul warned Timothy about this: 'For the time will come when
people will not tolerate sound doctrine but, following their own
desires and insatiable curiosity, will accumulate teachers and will
stop listening to the truth ....' (2 Timothy 4:3-4).

This does not mean that priests and other educators of adults are
attempting to deceive us. They are attempting to open our horizons
and to help us think about our faith. Therefore, we must take the

comments we read and hear and 'throw them into the hopper' of our conscience formation and consider them along with everything else we know and have experienced.

Recent popes and bishops have addressed a variety of issues, ranging from sexual issues to social issues, including peace, justice, the economy, and the dignity of women. We need to understand Church teachings on all of these subjects and deal with them on the basis of well-formed consciences.

As the world becomes more complex, the Gospel and our moral principles become more difficult to apply. No single person can provide all the moral guidance that we need to live as Christians today. That is why as Roman Catholics we should be grateful for the teaching office of the Church and the help that it provides us. We should be open to Church teachings and carefully examine what the Church asks of Christians today.

CHAPTER 5

What's in the Bible?

What is the Bible? How was the Bible written? What does the Bible tell us? One way to understand the Bible might be to compare it to a reflective diary or personal spiritual journal. For instance, if you were to describe in writing one significant religious experience in your life, you would need to reflect upon God's presence and activity in your life. Your response might be a simple statement or it might be a highly colourful and dramatic account of how God was present in your life. If you are a creative writer, you might write a long narrative or a beautiful poem. No matter what style you use, no matter how simple or complicated, the bottom line, the truth at the heart of your response, is that God has been active in your life.

Perhaps the event you choose to write about would be difficult to describe because God's presence and activity is usually beyond words. So, you might embellish the story or use analogies. You might say, 'I don't know exactly how to describe this, but it was like this...'

Sometimes the further away we are from an event, the more clouded the details become. The names of people and places may be forgotten or inaccurately stated. Other data may be in error, but we don't worry because the truth of the event still remains. Your response to a reflective question gives people some of your spiritual or religious history. This history is not like an autobiography in which there is concern about details. It is a special history that attempts to describe the mysterious workings of God in your life. The Bible is something like that.

The Bible is like a spiritual journal not just of a person but of a people. The Bible is salvation history, a religious history that is concerned not so much with the accuracy of names and events as with the truth of God's presence in human history and his desire to save people. The Bible uses a variety of writing styles to convey these truths, just as you might use a variety of styles in a personal spiritual journal.

If you kept a spiritual journal for a long period of time, you would be able to go back and see the development of your relationship with and understanding of God. Perhaps, as in almost any relationship, you would see the ups and downs, the joys and sorrows. Imagine a spiritual journal that covered almost two thousand years! That's what the Bible is like.

The events in the Bible were not recorded as eyewitness news stories. What is written in the Bible is usually the result of reflecting on events, remembering what others have said and done, and seeing in these events the saving power of God. This is something like your own reflection. You probably would not write about something happening today, for generally we are not fully aware of God's activity in the present. It is only as we look back upon an event that we can make sense of it and see how God was working in that event.

As Israel developed as a nation, the people looked back and said, 'Aha! That's what was happening. It was God who saved us.' They looked back to Abraham, Isaac, Jacob. They looked to their slavery in Egypt and to their leader, Moses, and they began to see a pattern of God's love and care. This looking back occurred over a long period of time. The stories of the patriarchs, the story of the Passover and exodus were told from generation to generation, passed along from tribe to tribe, told at campfires, celebrations and holidays. These stories made up the oral history of the Bible, which was passed on for a long time before the Bible was actually written.

In oral history, facts can become confused and altered. Imagine five people witnessing an accident. Each sees the accident from a different perspective and so each tells the story of the accident differently. But the truth remains. There was an accident. These five tell five others, and they in turn tell five more. Soon, the colours are changed, numbers are different, and other details about the accident are changed. But the truth remains. There was an accident. The story might be told from generation to generation, but the truth would remain. The oral tradition of the Bible is something like that. Names and places and other details might have changed before the stories were finally written, but the truth remained: God loves us; God saves us; we are God's chosen people!

Most of the Bible was written in a seven-hundred-year period between 600 B.C. and 100 A.D. It was written by many people in two basic languages, Hebrew and Greek. These writings were not in books but on scrolls. The Bible, therefore, is not so much one book as it is a collection of scrolls or books. It is like a miniature library containing seventy-three different books.

Imagine the Bible as a library building that has two floors. One floor is for the Old Testament, or Hebrew Scriptures, and the other floor is for the New Testament, or Christian Scriptures. And imagine that we can walk up and down the aisles of this library and browse among the different sections.

The first section in the Old Testament is the *Pentateuch* (five books), or the *Torah* (the law). These are the first five books of the Bible: Genesis, Exodus, Leviticus, Numbers and Deuteronomy. In them are found narratives, histories, census figures and descriptions of rituals, but most important are the laws, especially the laws of the Sinai covenant, which were given to Moses.

The second section of the Old Testament is commonly referred to as the *historical books*. While these books give us many insights into secular history, they are primarily intended to be religious histories. These books record one thousand years of history, from the events leading to the rise of the Davidic dynasty to the revolt of the Maccabees about one hundred years before the birth of Christ.

The third section of the Old Testament is called the *wisdom books* and contains books with a variety of styles, all of which are intended to provide instruction, or wisdom. Books in this category include the Book of Job, Psalms, Proverbs, Ecclesiastes, Song of Songs, Wisdom, and Ecclesiasticus, or Sirach.

The last section of the Old Testament is the *prophetic books*. The prophets were not fortune-tellers. They were mouth-pieces for the Lord, proclaiming God's word to an often stubborn and hard-hearted people. The prophets challenged people to change their sinful lives, and they promised God's loving mercy to those who would return to God with all their hearts. The prophets include some of the more well known, such as Isaiah and Jeremiah, and some of the lesser known, such as Zephaniah and Haggai.

The law and the prophets formed the most important parts of the Scriptures for the Hebrews. Jesus recognised this when he said, 'Do not think that I have come to abolish the law or the prophets. I have come not to abolish but to fulfill' (Matthew 5:17).

The second floor of the Bible library houses the books of the New Testament, or Christian Scriptures. The first part includes the four books of the Gospels (Good News). The four Gospels were written in a thirty-five year period between 65 and 100 A.D. Mark's Gospel was the first to be written and John's, the last. The Gospels were written in Greek, and each was written for a different audience with a slightly different approach or viewpoint.

The Gospels are not biographies of Jesus. They record the saving words and deeds of Jesus in order to show that Jesus was indeed the Messiah, the Saviour, who died and rose for our sins. The Gospels present a Jesus who challenged us to conversion, to a change in our lives, so that we might come to have full life with him.

After the Gospels come the Acts of the Apostles. This book, a history of the apostolic Church, records much of the missionary activity of Paul. Acts was written by Luke, the author of the third Gospel.

A large section of the New Testament consists of twenty-one letters, thirteen of which are attributed to Paul. These letters, written to Church communities and individuals, gave advice and encouragement and answered questions about the meaning of the Christian life. These letters were written before the Gospels.

The final book of the Bible is the Book of Revelation. This book uses images and symbols to describe the final victory of good over evil. It was intended to provide hope to a persecuted Church. Scripture scholars have yet to break the code for understanding all of the symbolism in this book.

The Bible is a special book. It is not just a book written by human beings, but one inspired by God. As we read in the Second Letter to Timothy, 'All scripture is inspired by God and is useful for teaching, for refutation, for correction, and for training in righteousness, so that one who belongs to God may be competent, equipped for every good work' (2 Timothy 3:16-17). God neither wrote the Bible personally nor did God, like a boss dictating a letter to a secretary, dictate every word of the Bible. God inspired its writers; that is, God opened the minds and hearts of people to let them see God's saving activity in history. Then God allowed them to express this knowledge in a variety of ways suited to almost any reading interest.

CHAPTER 6

How do we unlock the Bible's meaning?

Some people are afraid to read the Bible because of its size or because they fear misinterpreting it. How do you begin to read the Bible? The first step is to obtain an up-to-date translation that is approved by the Catholic Church. Three such translations are available: the Jerusalem Bible, the Revised Standard Version and the New American Bible. The Jerusalem Bible is the translation used in most Roman Catholic liturgies in this part of the world. It is good to have a personal copy of a Bible, and, no matter which Bible you use, it is good to be familiar with all of its features.

Examine the table of contents to get a sense of how the books of the Bible are arranged. The Old Testament comprises about the first three quarters of the Bible, with the New Testament being the last quarter. Find the place at which the New Testament begins. You will notice that in most Bibles the numbering of the pages in the New Testament begins anew, with page 1. Thus, there are two complete volumes in the Bible.

It is not necessary to memorise the table of contents, but you should have a general sense of the location of the books. Side tabs, which provide a thumb index for finding books, are available in many religious goods shops. The more you use the Bible, the easier it will become to locate books in the Bible. Don't become discouraged.

When the Bible was originally written, there were no chapters or other divisions in the books. Then many years ago, each book was divided into chapters, and almost each sentence was numbered as a verse for easy, universal reference. Thus, a reference such as Matthew 5:1-12 points all people to the same passage, the Beatitudes.

Matthew	5	1-12
Book of	Chapter	Verses
the Bible	(Colon or comma separates	
	chapter from verse)	

Sometimes a reference may look like this: Luke 5:1-11,17-26. This would indicate the Gospel of Luke, chapter 5, verses 1 to 11 and verses 17 to 26. The comma after the 11 indicates a break so that verses 12 to 16 are not included in this reference.

Other times a reference may look like this: 2 Corinthians 6:14 – 7:4. The 2 before Corinthians indicates the second letter to the Corinthians because there are a few books in the Bible that have more than one volume. This reference also has an elongated hyphen between the 14 and 7, indicating that this reference begins in the sixth chapter and continues into the seventh chapter. Again, don't be discouraged if you have difficulty finding a reference. The more you use your Bible, the easier it will become.

Other features in many Bibles are maps and charts. These are valuable for visualising the location of places that no longer exist or that now have different names.

A valuable feature in some Bibles is the Bible dictionary found at the back of the Bible. Although this is not a complete dictionary, it is a valuable guide for understanding major words and concepts.

Another feature of some Catholic Bibles is the listing for the three-year cycle of readings used in Sunday Masses. All cycles begin on the first Sunday of Advent, usually the last Sunday of November or first Sunday of December. Each year of the cycle is designated simply as A, B, or C. For instance, on the first Sunday of Advent in the year 1999, we will follow the readings for Cycle A. In 2000 we move to Cycle B, and in 2001 we will use Cycle C. In 2002 we start over with Cycle A.

There are three readings from the Bible in each Sunday's Liturgy. The first reading is usually from the Old Testament, the second is usually from one of the letters of the New Testament, and the third is always from a Gospel. The Gospels for Cycle A are generally from Matthew, most B's are from Mark, and C's are from Luke. John's Gospel is interspersed among the three cycles. The three-year cycle does not cover all of the Bible but highlights major doctrinal themes. The book of readings used in the Liturgy is called the Lectionary, which comes from a Latin word for 'readings'.

Another valuable feature in most good Bibles is a system of footnotes that can help you understand and interpret passages. Almost all Bibles have brief introductory articles for each book of the Bible. These usually give information about the author, date of composition, intended audience, and general theological message of the book. It is good to read these introductions, especially when you are reading a book for the first time.

Become familiar with your Bible and its features. These aids can enrich your understanding of the Bible and, in the long run, make the Bible easier to read.

How To Interpret a Passage

There are various levels of interpretation, various ways to understand a passage. For instance, the parable of the sower in Matthew 13 is about a farmer who sows seed, scattering it along the path, on rocks, in shallow ground and, finally, in good ground. Only the seed in the rich soil produces a good harvest. The face value or literal meaning is that a farmer will get the best crop from planting in the richest soil.

But there is another level of meaning to this parable. Jesus used it to explain the word of God. The seed is like the word, and people are like the places where the seed lands. Some people are hard-hearted, like the beaten path or rocks. Others are like shallow soil, having little depth to nourish the word. Others live among weeds, the cares and concerns of this world that choke the word. But there are people who are receptive to the word and nourish the word with good spiritual lives. These people are like the good soil where the word grows and flourishes. This was the meaning Jesus intended. We know that because the parable is one of the few Jesus explained for us.

A third way to understand the passage is at the personal level. What does this passage mean for me? When the word is planted in me, am I too hard, too shallow, or too distracted for it to thrive in me? This personal reflection is done prayerfully. Homilies and Bible study groups can help people reflect on the passage's meaning and apply it to their lives.

A note on a fundamentalist approach to the Bible: generally, the fundamentalist places greater emphasis on the first level of meaning, the literal level. This approach ignores placing a passage in context. It ignores biblical scholarship about literary styles, authorship, and audience. In a fundamentalist approach, every word of the Bible is taken literally. It is difficult to dialogue with a fundamentalist because the fundamentalist is not open to biblical research and scholarship, which can help unlock the real meaning of the passage.

However, the other extreme, in which the Bible is given only a personal or a symbolic meaning, must also be avoided. Catholics rely on the authority of the Church to provide a correct interpretation of the Scriptures. The Church's teaching office engages the assistance of its biblical scholars to assist it in this task.

Where Do You Begin?

Some people like to read the Bible from cover to cover, beginning with the book of Genesis. Others begin with the New Testament, more familiar material, and read a Gospel at a time. Others read selected passages, like the Sunday readings. The important thing is not quantity, but quality – how well you read a passage and reflect on what difference it makes in your life.

Here are some easy steps to follow after selecting a starting place:

• Set aside time to read, either by yourself or with your family. Keep the appointment. It takes discipline to continue reading the Bible.

• Read a passage once; then re-read it, checking footnotes and other references. Then read it for a third time, asking yourself, What does this passage mean for me? Underline or highlight passages that have special meaning for you.

• Keep a notebook or journal so that you can write questions or personal thoughts about a passage.

• If a Bible study group is available in your parish, join it so that you can learn more about the Bible.

• If you are a catechist, use the Bible in your class as part of a prayer service or as part of the instruction.

• Be patient with yourself and be open to the word of God in your life. The more you read, the more you will come to know and understand God's great love for you.

CHAPTER 7

What is the RCIA?

RCIA stands for 'Rite of Christian Initiation of Adults'. The RCIA revives the process that the early Church used to prepare adults to become Catholics.

Before the RCIA was revived, most non-Catholics who wished to become Catholic went through a series of classes or private instructions, usually with a priest. These were simply referred to as 'convert instructions'. Each week the convert read a chapter from a book and met in a private session with the priest, who would explain the Catholic doctrine. The number of sessions involved could be as few as three or as many as twenty-five or more.

After a period of study, the convert would be received into the Church. The reception was usually private. There was no community involvement in the person's preparation or in the person's reception into the Church. Most Catholics were unaware that anything special was happening.

With the revival of the RCIA, much has changed. First, the RCIA is a public affair. The rites that celebrate a person's progression along the journey of conversion are attended by and with the entire community. The rites are celebrated not only for the individual person, but for everyone, as reminders of their continuing faith journey.

Second, not only does the entire faith community help celebrate the rites, but the community is also actively involved in preparing the candidates for initiation into the Church. Members of the faith community act as co-ordinators, catechists, and sponsors. Although it is impossible for every person to be individually involved in this process, the entire community is asked to support the candidates with prayers and to help welcome them into the community.

Third, as part of this public and communal aspect of the RCIA, candidates share with one another in this process. In the past, a priest may have been instructing more than one person at the same time, but each person met individually with the priest, and the people being instructed did not get to know one another. In the RCIA many candidates share in the process and benefit from sharing with and supporting one another in the process.

Finally, a major difference between the previous convert instructions and the RCIA is the process used to prepare people for full acceptance into the Church. Emphasis in the past was on *instruction*. The emphasis in the RCIA is on *process*. The RCIA is a *process of conversion*. This process does not mean simply changing religions or choosing to join a certain religion. Rather, it involves a deep internal change of attitude and belief, which, in turn, leads to a radical change of life-style. This conversion process means that a person reflects on the Gospels, modeling his or her life on the life and teaching of Jesus. When a person's life is redirected and conformed to the Gospel teachings, the person has changed, has 'converted'.

The conversion process eventually leads a person to live as a full member of the Catholic faith community. Thus, it is necessary for a person also to know something about the Catholic Church and its teachings. In other words, the conversion process involves the head as well as the heart.

One of the difficulties in understanding the RCIA is the fact that it has retained many awkward names from the past. For instance, the first stage in the process is called *inquiry*. In this stage people are 'shopping around' or 'just looking'. During this time the Church simply opens its doors and says, 'Come and see! Take all the time you want. We'll be happy to answer your questions.' A spirit of warmth, welcoming, and hospitality prevails.

When a person has finished inquiring and has decided to begin the process of becoming Catholic, the person enters the stage known as the *catechumenate*. *The Rite of Becoming a Catechumen* is celebrated to begin this stage. During the catechumenate, the catechumens reflect intently upon the Gospel and examine various aspects of Catholicism. At the beginning of this stage, the catechumen is matched with a parish sponsor. A sponsor is a fully initiated adult Catholic, one who has been baptised and confirmed and who has received Holy Communion. The sponsor serves as companion on the journey, someone who walks with the catechumen, shares faith, and teaches by word and action what it means to be a Catholic.

During the catechumenate, the catechumens and their parish sponsors attend regular formal sessions together. These sessions may be conducted every week or every other week. Sometimes the sessions are conducted on a Sunday, with participants being invited to attend the Liturgy of the Word and being dismissed after the homily. Sponsors attend all of the sessions with their catechumens and find their own participation to be an enriching and rewarding experience. It is a privilege and an honour to serve as a parish sponsor.

Various activities are a part of the faith journey during the catechumenate. There are presentations and discussions, communal prayer and private prayer, reflection, group sharing and one-on-one sharing between sponsor and candidate. The important aspect of this stage is that participants see themselves led by God on a faith journey during which God is revealed.

Around Ash Wednesday or on the first Sunday of Lent, the candidates celebrate the *Rite of Election*. This election is not an occasion to cast votes but a time to recognise that the catechumens have indeed been numbered among God's chosen or elect. There is an opportunity in this rite for any member of the faith community to testify to the goodness and faith of any candidate.

With the celebration of the Rite of Election, the candidates enter a period known as *purification and enlightenment*. Occurring during Lent, this is the candidates' time to be on retreat and to fast and pray in preparation for their full entrance into the Church at the Easter Vigil. During this time the rest of the community prays and fasts for the candidates as a way of encouraging them and supporting them. During Lent the candidates celebrate three *scrutinies*, which are simply special prayers to help them reflect on their weaknesses and obtain healing. Also, during this time the catechumens are formally presented with the Creed and the Lord's Prayer.

Lent ends with the celebration of the most beautiful of all the Liturgies, the Easter Vigil. Some people shy away from this Liturgy because of its length. But it lasts no longer than an average football match! This Liturgy begins in darkness, which represents the death of the tomb, and moves to the lighting of the Easter fire and Easter or Paschal candle, which signifies the resurrection of Christ. Gradually, the entire Church is filled with light amid joyous shouts of 'Alleluia!' and the music of the Gloria.

During the Vigil Mass those catechumens who were never baptised are baptised in the newly blessed baptismal water. The newly baptised and the previously baptised, whether in the Catholic tradition or in another Christian tradition, are confirmed. All receive Holy Communion for the first time. Thus, all three sacraments of initiation – Baptism, Confirmation and Eucharist – are celebrated at one time. The Easter Vigil is an opportunity for all Catholics to renew their baptismal promises and to celebrate joyously their new life in the resurrected Christ.

But the celebration of the sacraments of initiation is not the end of the RCIA journey. The final stage is called *mystagogia*, a Greek word that means 'revealing of the mysteries'. During this time the *neophytes* (new Catholics) reflect on what they have just celebrated to come to a deeper understanding of their new faith. Although this period formally lasts from Easter to Pentecost, it actually lasts a lifetime, as we all continually grow in understanding the meaning of Christ's great love for us and in realising what our response should be. This is the on-going aspect of conversion. It never ends. Christ continually calls us to new levels of love.

Although the RCIA is intended primarily for non-Catholics, the process of journeying in the faith is one that all of us make over and over as we listen to the Gospel, reflect on our lives, and come to new understandings of how we should live. Thus, the RCIA presents a model process for many other formation processes in the Church.

CHAPTER 8

Evangelising – is it a Catholic thing to do?

Evangelisation calls to mind different images for different people. Some think of people who go door to door, distributing pamphlets. Others think of radio and television preachers who seem to work themselves into a frenzy as they berate audiences for their sinfulness and call people forth to personally accept Jesus Christ as their Lord and Saviour. Still others may think of tents and revival meetings on hot summer nights. In short, evangelisation does not often seem to be associated with Catholicism.

Yet evangelising is at the heart of the mission of the Church and, therefore, is indeed a very Catholic thing to do. To evangelise is to proclaim the Good News, or Gospel. The command to evangelise was one of the earliest that Jesus gave his apostles. 'He summoned the Twelve and gave them power and authority over all demons and to cure diseases, and he sent them to proclaim the kingdom of God and to heal [the sick]' (Luke 9:1-2). And this command to evangelise was also one of the last things Jesus said. 'All power in heaven and on earth has been given to me. Go, therefore, and make disciples of all nations, baptising them in the name of the Father, and of the Son, and of the Holy Spirit, teaching them to observe all that I have commanded you' (Matthew 28:18-20). Thus, evangelisation is indeed a very Catholic activity and should be at the heart of what every Catholic is doing.

One of the first things the Church did when it was empowered by the Holy Spirit was to evangelise. On Pentecost, Saint Peter stood up boldly before the people of Jerusalem and proclaimed the Good News. He evangelised and made some three thousand converts in one day! The missionary activities of the apostles, especially of Saint Paul, were dramatic examples of evangelisation. Throughout Church history we have seen and heard about the evangelising exploits of saints such as Patrick, Cyril and Methodius, Francis Xavier, Rose of Lima and Elizabeth Ann Seton, to name just a few.

Perhaps one reason Catholics have not seen evangelisation as an activity involving all Catholics is that we have tended to equate evangelisation with missionary activity. For most Catholics missionary implies making converts in foreign countries that have steaming jungles and exotic cultures. This may be one very limited aspect, but it is not the total picture of evangelisation.

The Second Vatican Council gave renewed emphasis to evangelisation, but it is the letter of Pope Paul VI entitled *On Evangelisation in the Modern World* that stands as the hallmark reflection on evangelisation in today's Catholic Church. In this letter Pope Paul called for the Church to bring the Good News into 'all the strata of humanity' (article 18). But where do we begin?

Evangelisation begins with proclaiming the Gospel to active Catholics. Why begin with the active? Evangelisation arouses faith, stirs it up, and gets people excited about their faith. Even the most active Catholic needs to be renewed in order to be able to go out and be a good evangeliser.

Evangelisation of the active involves a renewal of faith, and there are numerous ways to accomplish this. But the task is not as easy as it may seem. Certainly the sacraments, especially the Eucharist, provide renewal for people. But how many people really seem more excited about their faith after Mass than they did before? How many parishes have conducted Lenten missions or days of reflection or offered renewal programmes and had only a small percentage of the active participate? Thus, renewing active Catholics is one of the first challenges of evangelisation.

The next group within the Church in need of evangelisation consists of inactive Catholics. These are Catholics who may go to church weekly but are otherwise not involved in the parish. Or they may not even go weekly but still consider themselves very much Catholic. They may enroll their children in the parish school but are not otherwise seen in the parish. They may give a variety of reasons for their inactivity, and they may even express a wish to 'go more often' but are generally content with their inactive status. 'God understands,' is their motto.

Evangelising this group does not mean preaching to them. Evangelisation can be as simple as parishioners providing a Sunday nursery or child care so that adults can attend Mass and other parish activities. Sometimes all that is needed is a friendly invitation to come along to a programme or to join an activity. Some people may be inactive simply because they are shy and need to feel welcomed and comfortable. Some people say that they are inactive because it doesn't seem to make any difference how active anyone is: 'You go to church every Sunday and I don't see much difference in your life!' There is nothing more powerful in Catholic evangelisation than the example of good lives lived by those who are Catholic.

Alienated Catholics are another group of people in need of evangelisation. These are people who were baptised in the Catholic faith, but who stopped participating in the Church because of some misunderstanding or tremendous hurt. They may say that they stopped for any number of reasons:
- 'The priest refused to bury my mother.'
- 'The priest wouldn't baptise my daughter.'
- 'My father lost his job and couldn't afford to contribute.'
- 'I don't agree with the Church's teaching on...'
- 'The Church is too liberal.'
- 'The Church is too conservative.'
- 'The Church is filled with hypocrites...'

The alienated are a difficult group to evangelise because they are filled with deep pain and hurts. There is little sense in trying to reason with them, for logic alone will not bring the alienated back. These people often need the opportunity to be heard, to tell their stories, to be supported and aided in the process of returning to the Church. The Christian witness and pastoral sensitivity of everyone in the faith community is important in facilitating the healing process.

Another group may include some of our neighbours, friends, and co-workers. These are searching people who may or may not have been baptised. In many cases they did not have much background in a faith or, if they did, they have not practised their faith for a long time. They have questions such as, 'Isn't there more to life?' 'What is my ultimate purpose in life?' 'What can give me the greatest happiness?' They may have wondered about such things but are unsure where or to whom to turn for answers.

Simple invitations often are all that searching people need. They just need someone to say, 'Come with me.' Parish open houses and personal invitations are first steps to evangelising people who are searching.

Stealing members from other religious groups or Churches is not the purpose of Catholic evangelisation. Evangelisation should not be argumentative or confrontational. Catholic evangelisation should be respectful of other religious beliefs. But respect does not necessarily mean agreement. Catholic evangelisation should be characterised by warmth, hospitality, and invitation. 'Come and see' (John 1:46).

A person does not have to be a preacher, teacher, or even a good speaker in order to evangelise, for the proclamation of the Gospel is only one dimension of evangelisation. Evangelisation occurs not only through words but also through actions. The Church evangelises through hospitals established to care for the sick and injured. It evangelises through shelters and meal-on-wheels designed to assist the homeless and hungry. The Church evangelises through schools founded to educate the young.

Evangelisation can take place in the most common places. We evangelise at work when we do an honest day's work for a day's pay. We evangelise when we are honest in our business dealings and when we are fair to fellow employees. We evangelise when we say, 'I care' by offering sympathy and help to a neighbour in need. We evangelise not just when we preach the Good News but when we *are* Good News.

Evangelisation is at the centre of the mission of the Church. To be a Catholic is to be an evangeliser; that is, we are to bring the Good News of Jesus Christ to every person we meet. To do less is to fail in being fully Catholic Christians and disciples of Jesus Christ.

CHAPTER 9

Social Issues – should the Church be involved?

The Church exists in order to bring about the kingdom of God. Thus, by its very nature, the Church works to transform creation into a state of peace and love. The Church's mission is to be deeply involved in the world and with people. While the Church's mission is a spiritual one, it accomplishes its work in the social order.

Also, the Church itself is a social institution. It is comprised of people who gather in an organised fashion with a particular leadership structure and who meet certain requirements for membership. As a social organisation, the Church is an active participant in the affairs of the world. It is an active economic participant. It owns land and buildings. It hires people. If its individual churches, schools, hospitals, cemeteries and other holdings were gathered together as one corporation, it might well be the world's largest conglomerate.

As a social participant, the Church is involved in government affairs. The Catholic Church, with its headquarters in the Vatican, comprises one of the world's smallest governments, yet it is one of the most influential. The Vatican has diplomatic relations and ties with other world governments. The Catholic Church cannot be ignored as a social institution, and it cannot help being involved in social issues and affairs. The question is, How much should the Church be involved?

Religion is not a private affair, something existing solely between an individual and God. Religious belief leads to action; love for God is expressed in love for others. 'If anyone says, "I love God," but hates his brother, he is a liar; for whoever does not love a brother whom he has seen cannot love God whom he has not seen. This is the commandment we have from him: whoever loves God must also love his brother' (1 John 4:20-21).

Jesus' teachings were concerned with people, especially the poor and oppressed. The Beatitudes, for example, address social issues that are relevant for any age:

Blessed are the poor in spirit...
Blessed are they who mourn...
Blessed are the meek...
Blessed are they who hunger and thirst for righteousness...
Blessed are the merciful...
Blessed are the clean of heart...
Blessed are the peacemakers....
(Matthew 5:3-9).

In Luke's Gospel, we read that, as Jesus began his ministry, he applied the words of Isaiah to himself:
The Spirit of the Lord is upon me,
because he has anointed me
to bring glad tidings to the poor.
He has sent me to proclaim liberty to captives
and recovery of sight to the blind,
to let the oppressed go free,
and to proclaim a year acceptable to the Lord
(Luke 4:18) (See also Isaiah 61:1-2).

Considering that almost any government might be threatened by those statements, it is amazing that Jesus wasn't killed on the spot!

In the end we will be judged not just on the depth of our faith but on our response to the needs of others, that is, on our social involvement. Jesus demands such involvement from us:
For I was hungry and you gave me food, I was thirsty and you gave me drink, a stranger and you welcomed me, naked and you clothed me, ill and you cared for me, in prison and you visited me (Matthew 25:35-36).

Thus, it should really be no surprise that the Church speaks on social issues and is involved in them. However, while the Church has always preached the Gospel, only within the past hundred years has it developed its social doctrines, that is, applied the Gospel to social issues. That the Catholic Church was late in developing these doctrines is not surprising when we understand its history.

For the first four hundred years of its existence, the Church was concerned with getting established. It had to defend itself from persecutions and, for the most part, it was an underground and out-lawed organisation.

During the next four hundred years, the Church developed its theological doctrines and spent much of its energy correcting heresies. Society itself was in disarray during the Dark Ages.

From 800 to 1500, the Church and the state were so intimately connected that, in many cases, the Church would have been condemning itself if it had addressed some of the injustices in society. It was an age in which the Church needed to remove the plank from its own eye before removing the splinter from anyone else's.

After the Reformation the Catholic Church became introverted and concerned about its own internal affairs. Yet, while it was introspective, the Catholic Church was also involved in some of its greatest missionary activity as new worlds were being discovered.

Pope Leo XIII's encyclical, *The Condition of Labour (Rerum Novarum)*, perhaps marks the entrance of the Catholic Church into a systematic formulation of social doctrines. Written in 1891, this was the first labour encyclical. It stressed the dignity of the worker and addressed some of the ills caused by the industrial revolution. Concerned about the dignity and welfare of all people, the Pope spoke as the primary teacher of the Church. Pope Leo's encyclical was an attempt to apply the teachings of the Gospel to a new structure in society, modern industry.

The world did not come to a grinding halt because of Pope Leo's encyclical. Change comes slowly. Since the time when *Rerum Novarum* was written, other popes have written major statements on social issues. Among the more recent would be Pope John XXIII's *Peace on Earth (Pacem in Terris)*, Pope Paul VI's *On The Development of Peoples (Populorum Progressio)*, and Pope John Paul II's *On Social Concern (Sollicitudo Rei Socialis)*. These letters are attempts to apply the Gospel to major world issues such as justice, equality, concern for the poor, freedom, disarmament, and so forth. The popes do not write as military, political or economic experts. They write as moral teachers.

Why do the popes and bishops write and speak out on social issues? Some people might say that the popes and bishops should be concerned only with religion. Religion, however, cannot be separated from the rest of life. In an important document on the role of the Church, the bishops at the Second Vatican Council stated, 'At all times the Church carries the responsibility of reading the signs of the time and of interpreting them in the light of the Gospel...' (*Pastoral Constitution on the Church in the Modern World*, article 4).

The world of the past hundred years is totally different from that of previous times. The world has shrunk. Our global dependency has expanded the meaning of *neighbour* beyond national boundaries. The threat of instant annihilation through a nuclear holocaust, the domination of superpowers over other countries, the disproportionate distribution of the earth's resources and the misuse of those resources, along with many other modern issues, require a moral guidance that is unprecedented in human and religious history. Thus, there is a definite need for the teaching authority of the Church, for the popes and bishops, to speak on these complex issues.

But it is not enough for the Church to simply address contemporary issues. All Catholics, because of their Baptism, are required to be actively involved in bringing about the kingdom of God, a kingdom of peace and justice. In the Vatican II document on the laity, the bishops called upon lay people, because of their special position in the world, to be actively involved in transforming the world according to God's plan. It is not enough to simply pray our way into heaven. As Jesus said, 'Not everyone who says to me, "Lord, Lord," will enter the kingdom of heaven, but only the one who does the will of my Father in heaven' (Matthew 7:21).

We cannot separate what we believe from what we do every day. We cannot hear the Gospel parable of the good Samaritan on Sunday and drive past the homeless, the hungry and abused on Monday without responding to their needs. We cannot sing songs of peace in church and then support governments that build up arms or support terrorists or use violence to accomplish their goals. We cannot receive the Bread of Life and then let forty thousand children die each day in the world because of starvation and related diseases.

We are the Church, the Body of Christ. Should the Church be involved in social issues? We are commanded to care for others and

to be involved. We cannot separate our religion from our daily
lives.

What good is it, my brothers, if someone says he has faith but
does not have works? Can that faith save him? If a brother or sister
has nothing to wear and has no food for the day, and one of you
says to them, 'Go in peace, keep warm, and eat well,' but you do
not give them the necessities of the body, what good is it? So also
faith of itself, if it does not have works, is dead (James 2:14-17).

We must be involved in social affairs.

CHAPTER 10

What's so special about the Sacraments?

One of the special privileges of being Catholic is being able to participate in the sacramental life of the Church. In the sacraments we have unique opportunities to encounter God personally. Yet, for many Catholics, the sacraments seem to have lost their vitality. The sacraments are often approached as routine celebrations rather than as the life-giving forces they are. Or, even worse, as sometimes may be the case in Baptisms, first Communions and Marriages, the sacraments are celebrated more as extravagant social functions than as spiritual events. What's so special about the sacraments? That is often a question raised by young people, and they probably ask it because their parents and teachers haven't given them satisfactory answers. Here's one way to answer that question.

Imagine a rolled-up parchment tied with a silk ribbon. Some people may see it only as rolled paper tied with ribbon. Others may see it as an important document. However, those who know the struggle involved in getting an education can recognise the parchment as a diploma. They give this rolled paper new meaning.

A diploma is a sign of graduation, but it is not graduation. The diploma represents achievement and accomplishments, but the graduate would still have all the achievements and accomplishments without the diploma. The diploma serves as a symbol to help others readily understand what is inside of us.

Diplomas are presented in graduation exercises. There are elaborate ceremonies that mark the giving of a diploma. These ceremonies are the way we acknowledge our achievements. Graduation ceremonies allow others to understand what is happening in our lives. They bring others together to celebrate our accomplishments. But we could graduate without a graduation exercise, and we could even accomplish a certain amount of learning without receiving a diploma. The diploma and the graduation exercise are tangibles that express an intangible. They point out our accomplishments, but they are not the accomplishments in themselves.

Because we are human, we need diplomas and graduations. We need signs like the diploma so that we and others can see the unseen, and we need celebrations like the graduation exercise so that others can share in our joy. In other words, we need sacraments (signs) and rituals (celebrations).

If you are still not sure, consider this. How do little children know that their parents love them? Sure, they feel safe and secure when they have a roof over their heads and when they have sufficient food to eat. But they really come to know that they are loved when they are hugged and embraced.

A child may very well be loved without being hugged and embraced, and a child may even know that he or she is loved without the hugs. But hugs and embraces are generally seen as essential to establishing feelings of self-worth, esteem, and love, and they provide the basis for entering into deep, personal relationships. Let's face it, we all need to be hugged once in a while!

Hugs are more than symbols of being loved. They are not just things, like a diploma. Hugs are actions that express outwardly the inward reality of love. Hugs are not only something we get but something we give. As we are receiving a hug, we are also giving one. Hugs make us one with another as the other becomes one with us. They help us share our lives with another.

For those old enough to remember, the catechism definition of a sacrament may come to mind here: 'A sacrament is an outward sign, instituted by Christ, to give grace.' More simply put, sacraments are God's way of hugging us!

Sometimes Catholics lose sight of the sacraments and the great love that is contained in them. We look only upon the signs and tend to see the sacraments as things. The sacraments become like the diploma, the sign of accomplishment, when we have forgotten the late nights of study and the struggle to get an education. Just as there is more to a diploma than a rolled-up sheet of paper, there is more to the sacraments than meets the eye.

If sacraments are signs of God's love for us, then the greatest sign is Jesus Christ. But Jesus isn't around physically to hug us. So, through the Church, we can experience God's love for us and express our love for God in seven special ways. These are the seven sacraments.

In the seven sacraments God shows love for us at special times in our lives:

- When we begin our new lives as Christians, God pours on us the refreshing waters of Baptism.
- When we are ready to affirm the faith we received in Baptism, God anoints us with the chrism of Confirmation.
- When we need nourishment, God gives us the bread of Eucharist.
- When we fail, God shows us forgiveness with the sacrament of Reconciliation.
- When we are in need of healing, God comforts us with the Anointing of the Sick.
- When we choose either to marry or to enter the priesthood, God is present to us in Marriage or in Holy Orders.

Celebrating the sacraments is something like participating in a graduation exercise. Both activities celebrate past events or accomplishments. Both activities require preparation in the past for a celebration to occur in the present.

Then there is the present moment of each event. In graduation a diploma is conferred. It happens quickly, but it is the main ritual act of graduating. So in each of the sacraments there is a central present moment – the pouring of water, the anointing with oil, the eating of the bread and drinking from the cup, and so on.

But there is also a future dimension to each activity. Graduation is commonly referred to as commencement, which means 'beginning'. In graduation we celebrate the past in a present moment of signs and symbols, and we immediately move on to the future, to continue our education or to get a job. So, too, the sacraments have a futuristic thrust as they compel us to live in new ways, filled with the life-giving force of God. After graduation our lives are never the same. After we celebrate a sacrament, our lives should never be the same, either.

It is important to realise that the sacraments are not magical. The sacraments are deep expressions of love and faith. We must understand what we are doing and be receptive to God's love. But even if we are not entirely open, something still happens to us. It is like being hugged even when we don't feel like being hugged. The warmth of the other's embrace is almost enough to make us return the hug. Have you ever hugged a stubborn, pouting child? The child is stiff and offers no response. But hold the child long enough and squeeze hard enough, and eventually you'll get a hug in return. God must view us sometimes as stubborn and pouting children. But, fortunately, God never lets go of us.

Some people claim that they don't need to celebrate the sacraments. Their excuse is that they know that God loves them. But imagine two friends or two lovers who never express their love for each other because 'the other person knows that I love him or her.' That relationship probably will not last very long. Imagine a parent who would say to a young child, 'I don't need to hug you because you should know that I love you!' No loving parent would do that. We are children of God, and as any child would, we all need God's hugs.

When people brought their children to Jesus, he did not preach to them. He did not say, 'I am Jesus and you know how much I love you.' Instead, 'he embraced them and blessed them' (Mark 10:16).

Are the sacraments special? Indeed they are!

Have you been hugged by God lately?

CHAPTER 11

The Mass – what really happens?

The Eucharist is a sacrificial meal, not just a sacrifice and not just a meal. It seems that recently we have placed greater emphasis on the Mass, or celebration of the Eucharist, as a meal. However, both the sacrificial and meal dimensions of the Eucharist have been and continue to be essential, even if one dimension happens at certain times to receive greater attention.

The sacrificial aspect of the Eucharist has deep roots in Jewish religious practice. When Jesus instituted the Eucharist, he was celebrating the Jewish Passover. In the Passover a lamb was slain, and its blood was smeared on the doorposts of the Israelites who were captive in Egypt. The angel of death came over the land and struck down the first-born in each house that did not have the blood smeared on its doorposts, that is, each house of the Egyptians. Thus, by the blood of the sacrificed lamb, the first-born of all the Israelites were spared, and it was this event that ultimately resulted in the release of the Israelites from their slavery in Egypt.

Jesus is the Lamb of God. It is by his blood that each of us is saved. By his blood each of us is freed from the bondage of sin and allowed to share our new life with God. This is the new Passover that is celebrated in the Eucharist. Jewish people celebrate the Passover once a year and remember their deliverance from slavery. Catholic Christians celebrate the new Passover in each Eucharist and not only recall their release from sin but actually experience the forgiveness of sins again and again.

Jesus told his disciples at the Last Supper, 'This cup is the new covenant in my blood...' (Luke 22:20). What was the old covenant and how was it celebrated? Generally, the covenant ceremonies found in the Hebrew Scriptures required the sacrifice of an animal. Part of the animal's blood was splashed on the altar as a sign of God's involvement in the covenant, and the other half of the blood was splashed on the people as a sign of their sharing in the covenant. For the Israelites, blood was a powerful symbol of life.

Therefore, the sharing of blood, as indicated in the splashing, meant that both parties of the covenant were bound together.

After Moses received the Ten Commandments and all the other laws associated with them, he asked the Israelites if they would accept the laws. They agreed to accept them, and thus they entered into a covenant with God. Moses directed the leaders to sacrifice a bull, and its blood was splashed on the altar and on the people. This was the making of the old covenant, based upon the Israelites' acceptance of God's laws and sealed with the ritualistic sacrifice of an animal.

In the new covenant that Christ makes with us, we are asked to accept not only a set of laws but also the very life-style that Christ himself has shown us. In the making of this new covenant, the covenant-maker, Christ, becomes the victim and offers himself up to God. We are, however, not splashed with Christ's blood; we are commanded to actually drink his blood and to eat his flesh made present in the Eucharist. Thus, we can truly become one with Christ in this covenant, not just ritually but actually.

The making of this new covenant is not a single ritual event. It involves the covenant meal, the sacrifice of the victim on the cross, and the celebration of Christ's new life in the resurrection. The Eucharist, then, should be seen in terms of Holy Thursday, Good Friday and Easter Sunday. All of these events are celebrated in the Eucharist.

When we celebrate the Eucharist, Christ does not die upon the cross the way he did on that first Good Friday. Our Eucharist is not a barbaric re-enactment of Christ's crucifixion. Christ died once and for all. But each Eucharist is an extension of that sacrifice so that each person, in every age and place, can fully and actively participate in that sacrifice in which Christ gave up his life for our sins. When we celebrate Eucharist, the covenant is re-established with us.

Saint Paul tells us, 'For as often as you eat this bread and drink the cup, you proclaim the death of the Lord until he comes' (1 Corinthians 11:26). In each Eucharist we participate fully in the death and resurrection of the Lord just as if we had been present at those events almost two thousand years ago. Yes, the Mass is still a sacrifice and, in it, we become united with the priest and victim, Christ. Because of our union with him, we are also asked to offer ourselves up totally to God.

But at the same time, the Eucharist is a sacrificial meal, a banquet in which all believers are brought together to share in the Body of Christ in order more fully to become the Body of Christ. What is accomplished in the Eucharist should immediately draw us to give great praise. We are saved! We are a new people! Christ lives among us! Therefore, our Eucharistic celebration should be filled with singing and praising God for all that God has done for us. Matthew even records that the disciples sang a hymn after the celebration of the first Eucharist (Matthew 26:30).

Our altar, our place of sacrifice, is also a table, for it was around a table that Jesus gathered his disciples and shared his very life with them. Thus, it is around the table that we are fed and nourished with the life of Christ.

The celebration of the Eucharist should not be a sombre event. It would be very sombre if Christ had died and that had been the end of everything. But we gather in joy because of the resurrection: '... if Christ has not been raised, your faith is vain' (1 Corinthians 15:17). Christ is alive! That is indeed good news, and our celebration should reflect that good news.

The Eucharistic celebration is a communal event. It is interesting to note that the term *Body of Christ* refers not only to the physical presence of Christ in the Eucharist but also to the total presence of Christ in the Church. We are the Body of Christ, for all of us become that Body because of the Body of Christ that we receive. Therefore, our attention should be given to what is happening to all of us in the Eucharist.

The Eucharist is a meal, a new Passover meal. In the Passover celebration there is the recounting of the story of salvation, God is praised and thanked, and toasts are drunk in memory of those events. It is a festive occasion. That is how the first new Passover was celebrated. It would be difficult to imagine the apostles pulling out their prayer books or rosaries and praying silently during that meal, while Jesus was excitedly recounting the story of salvation.

And only one left the celebration early, the one who betrayed Christ.

Our Eucharistic meal should be something like the one that the apostles celebrated with Jesus. It should be filled with songs and prayers. It should be filled with the proclamation of the ways God loves us, and we should attentively listen to those words. And all should be gathered into the Body of Christ by receiving that Body since Jesus told us that we should take and eat.

Jesus also told us to drink from the cup. In today's Eucharistic celebrations we have once again been given the option of drinking from the cup. Some people have fears about drinking for health reasons, and others simply find it awkward. It is not necessary to drink from the cup in order to receive the total presence of Christ, for Christ is truly and totally present in the bread alone. Christ is also truly and totally present in the wine alone. The practice of drinking from the cup has been restored as a fuller sign of our oneness with Christ. We should do whatever we feel comfortable doing.

In the Eucharist, the sacrificial meal, we make our new covenant with God through Jesus Christ. We accept the life-style that Christ has shown us. Thus, when we leave the Eucharistic celebration, our lives should be different – we should be ready to live according to the new covenant of love.

CHAPTER 12

Is anything sinful any more?

In the past, understanding what was and what was not sinful was relatively simple. Sin was an offense against God. Anything that seemed to 'hurt God's feelings' was sinful.

How did a person know what offended God? Simple. Sin was viewed in highly legalistic terms. If a person broke a law or rule, such as one of the Ten Commandments or the Precepts of the Church, then that person sinned. Morality was a matter of keeping the rules, much as a person does in playing a game or driving a car. In a game, a person keeps track of fouls; and in driving a car, the number of traffic offence tickets, and then pays a penalty or fine. In Confession, a person reported his or her sins and did the assigned penance. Then, his or her 'slate' was cleared.

Sins were either venial or mortal. They were either minor offences or serious offences. Today, things just don't seem that simple. Is anything sinful today? Probably more than what we think.

One reason why we are confused about sin is that our understanding of our relationship with God has shifted. In the past we viewed God as someone 'out there', a ruler, a judge, a king who gave us rules to follow but surely someone who always loved us and forgave us if we were sorry and if we 'paid the fine.'

Today the emphasis is on 'God with us', God, who seems to be one of us. Perhaps we have moved too far in emphasising the love of God. God has become an easy God. Many people seem to say, 'It doesn't matter what I do. God forgives me and God loves me. God understands.' In short, we have simply taken God for granted.

To understand our relationship with God and, therefore, to understand love and sin in this relationship, it might be helpful to use an analogy. Our relationship with God is like the relationship of two people who get married. They are in love and express their love by committing their lives exclusively to each other in marriage. They pledge themselves totally to each other out of love, not because of a contract. In Baptism we, in a similar way, get 'married to God'. We pledge our lives to God. We enter into a relationship with God, just as a couple enter into a relationship with each other.

When we are baptised, we begin our life with God anew. Everything seems perfect. Nothing is going to spoil this relationship. We are like the young married couple. They believe that they have the perfect marriage and that nothing is going to disrupt it. But the honeymoon lasts only so long. Eventually, they enter into day-to-day living, and the hard work of the relationship begins.

Soon there are those little things that begin to irritate the relationship. He leaves the cap off the toothpaste. She has laundry hanging in the shower. He throws his socks in the corner and expects his wife to pick them up. And on and on. These things can begin to disturb the loving relationship. These little things are like sins. They are not legal infractions, but they are actions that deteriorate a relationship.

In a similar way our relationship with God sometimes begins to develop little cracks. We get careless in our relationship. We don't love others the way God wants us to. We begin to cheat and lie. We begin to take God for granted, as if to say, 'God will pick up our socks in the corner.' But if these little things are left unattended, the relationship is strained further and further.

You can almost see the deterioration in some marriage relationships. The couple communicate less and less. They complain about each other more and more. Their actions become less and less loving toward each other. More and more, they take each other for granted. Perhaps they spend less time with each other. Each time they fail to communicate, each time they fail to respect each other's feelings, each time they take each other for granted, they sin; that is, they weaken their relationship. They grow further and further apart, and they drift away from the ideal love that they professed on their wedding day.

Sometimes we are like this married couple in our relationship with God. We communicate with God less frequently in prayer. We don't read the Scriptures or carefully listen to their proclamation. Maybe we don't encounter God as frequently in the sacraments.

We fail to see God in others. We become unjust and unloving in our human relationships. In short, we take God for granted and move further and further away from the ideal love that we professed in Baptism. Sometimes our actions are sinful because they are infractions of rules. However, any action that weakens our relationship with God is always sinful. We have failed to continue to grow in our baptismal love. We have failed to love God who first loved us (1 John 4:19).

Previously in Catholic morality we tended to emphasise the negative and the legalistic. We asked, 'How far can I go before something is sinful?' instead of asking, 'What can I contribute to my relationship with God?' We tended to look at the minimum we could do and how much we could get away with, instead of looking at how our actions could strengthen our relationship with God. In a loving relationship we don't look at getting away with things. Rather, we look at how much we can do for the other person.

In one sense, Catholic morality is very simple. To judge an act, all we need to ask is, 'Does this act strengthen or weaken my relationship with God?' If it weakens the relationship, then it is sinful.

But how can we tell if something strengthens or weakens our love relationship with God? One way is to look at the ideal of this relationship, and that is found most perfectly in the relationship between Jesus and his Father. Therefore, the norm for judging ourselves should be Jesus – his life, his teaching, his ministry, his death because of his love for us.

Love is more than just avoiding certain actions. Love is more than not taking God's name in vain, not missing Mass, not talking back to parents, not killing, not committing adultery, not stealing, and not lying. As Jesus told the rich young man who had kept all the Commandments, 'You are lacking in one thing. Go, sell what you have, and give to [the] poor and you will have treasure in heaven' (Mark 10:21).

A loving relationship with God is built more on what we *do* than on what we avoid. 'This is how all will know that you are my disciples, if you have love for one another' (John 13:35).

Building a love relationship is hard work. It means that we must feed the hungry, visit the imprisoned, and shelter the homeless, as

Jesus commanded us in Matthew 25:31-46. It means that we must bring glad tidings to the poor, proclaim liberty to captives, give sight to the blind, and set the oppressed free, as Jesus proclaimed in Luke 4:18-19, when he quoted Isaiah 61:1-2.

When we fail to do these things, we are not strengthening our relationship with God; we are not expressing our love. Our relationship is weakened, and therefore we sin.

Most marriages which fail, fail, not because of an individual act, although one act may be the one that finally 'breaks the camel's back'. Most of them fail, however, because the partners let little things build up, because they fail to work at the relationship, because they fail to give themselves to each other totally, without question. Thus, in a similar way, our relationship with God does not suddenly fall apart without warning. Our relationship breaks because we fail to express our love for God on a daily basis. Saint Paul stresses the importance of our routine daily actions when he says, 'So whether you eat or drink, or whatever you do, do everything for the glory of God' (1 Corinthians 10:31).

Is anything sinful today? Yes, indeed! Today, perhaps even more than in the past, there should be a greater awareness of sin. Our emphasis in our moral lives should be on building our relationship with God, using Jesus as our model. To do anything less than to live a fully Christ-like life is sinful. So there is probably much more sin in our lives than we may want to admit.

CHAPTER 13

The sacrament of Penance – do we need it?

Many Catholics grew up with a fairly simple but often extremely fearful understanding and experience of the sacrament of Penance, or 'confession', as it was more popularly known. A person would begin by examining his or her conscience, often by going through a list of the Ten Commandments and keeping a running tab of the number of times he or she had broken a commandment, either in thought or deed. (It was sinful just thinking about killing your younger brother because he had listened in on your phone conversation with your girlfriend.) With the tally in mind a person would then enter the darkened confessional box, perspire greatly, and wait for the sliding door to open.

'Bless me, Father, for I have sinned. My last confession was...'

The person would enumerate the list of sins, speeding up or mumbling at points when he or she did not really want the priest to hear. The priest would offer his counsel and assign a penance (usually three Hail Marys and three Our Fathers). The person would say the Act of Contrition while, at the same time, seemingly in an attempt to confuse him or her, the priest would say the prayer of absolution. The person would walk out the door, remain in church long enough to say the penance, and leave with the knowledge that he or she was beginning with a clean slate.

This scenario oversimplifies the way many people went to confession, and it certainly is not intended to demean all the good people who received the sacrament as a means for truly changing their lives. But there have been some changes in the sacrament so that it is no longer a matter of just 'going to confession' but of celebrating reconciliation.

Today the sacrament is technically called the sacrament of Penance. However, penance describes only one part of the whole experience, and it is not adequate to describe the total event, just as confession was never an adequate term for the sacrament. Reconciliation is commonly used, but again, this simply describes the desired outcome. There are three rites, or ways of celebrating the sacrament, and these are known as the rites of reconciliation. Perhaps no word or phrase can adequately capture all that is involved in this sacrament.

Over the past number of years there has been a change in emphasis in the sacrament. We have moved from a numerical listing of offences to a process of conversion and a celebration of that conversion. Conversion is a word that was generally reserved for describing Protestants who wanted to become Catholic. But all Catholics are in need of conversion. Throughout our entire lives we convert and reconvert. Conversion means a radical, 180-degree turn in a person's life. In conversion we move from a sinful life to a God-oriented life.

Conversion is more than a recitation of a list of sins. Conversion means getting to the core of our being and finding the root of our sins – in our pride, selfishness, lack of faith, and so forth.

Conversion does not happen quickly. We struggle in the conversion process. We wrestle within our souls. We wonder whether we are doing the right thing. But when we decide to change, it is usually a long-lasting change, one that lasts longer than Saturday to Saturday.

The conversion process leads us to reconciliation. At one time our sinfulness was seen more as a private matter between God and us. Today, greater emphasis is placed on the social and communal dimensions of sin. I sin, but I sin against someone who is not only an individual but part of a community. There is truly no such thing as a private sin, for when I sin, I affect someone else. When I sin, I am less than what I could be in relationship to another. As Saint Paul says, if one part of the body suffers, the entire body suffers (1 Corinthians 12:26).

When I sin, it is sometimes difficult, if not impossible, to go to each person I have sinned against to receive that person's forgiveness. Thus, the priest serves as a representative of the community of the Church in facilitating this reconciliation. This does not diminish our personal responsibility, though, to actually reconcile ourselves with those we have sinned against and, if possible, to make restitution.

In reconciliation I see each person as a member of the Body of Christ, and I know that my sin has affected that person – my neighbour, the person next to me in the office, the person in the front pew and in the last pew. Nameless people, but people affected by my sin. Through reconciliation I am rejoined to all these people in the family of Christ.

One aspect of the sacrament of Penance that we sometimes find difficult to do is to *celebrate* the sacrament. In the past, when confessions were heard in hushed whispers in a darkened cubicle, there seemed to be little reason to celebrate. But there is!

Imagine going to a doctor and receiving the good news that the lump you worried about was not malignant. Imagine the joy in coming out of that office. There is something freeing in being given good news, and that's what happens to us in the sacrament of Penance. We are given good news: 'Go in peace. Your sins are forgiven.' We are free! We should jump for joy and celebrate!

Wouldn't it be great if parents threw as big a party for their children when the children celebrate their First Penance as the parents do when children celebrate their First Communion? In Penance we come to Jesus, like the prodigal son courageously making that journey back to the father. That is conversion. That is accomplishment. There is reason to rejoice and celebrate 'because this son of mine was dead, and has come to life again; he was lost, and has been found' (Luke 15:24).

The story of the prodigal son captures much of what is being celebrated in the sacrament of Penance today. After wasting his inheritance, the son converts, decides to change his life. His decision comes after he has experienced suffering and pain, after he has had to eat corn with pigs. Only then does he come to his senses and realise that he has sinned.

When the son decides to return, when he examines his conscience, he doesn't reflect on a numerical account of how he squandered the money. He doesn't say, 'I spent £2,000 on drinking and £5,000 on loose women and £10,000 on gambling.' Instead, he simply says, 'Father, I have sinned against heaven and against you; I no longer deserve to be called your son' (Luke 15:21). In other words, the son admits that his life was going in the wrong direction, and now he wants to turn it around. That is conversion. And that is confession.

It is interesting to note in the story of the prodigal son that even before the son confesses, his father waits for him and runs to embrace him and welcome him back. The father's concern was the son's conversion and return, not his confession. Yet, the son needs to express his conversion and his repentance: 'I no longer deserve to be called your son' (Luke 15:21).

A final aspect of the story is the celebrational aspect. The father orders a great feast to be celebrated in his son's honour. The father rejoices just as God rejoices at our return and just as the entire community should rejoice at our return. When we celebrate the sacrament of Penance, there should be more than just a good feeling of relief; there should be bells ringing and festive music playing!

Imagine what the son's experience would have been like if he had turned from his sinful ways and had seriously decided to change his life-style but had not encountered his loving father. He could well have assumed that his father would forgive him and he could have felt forgiven, but he would have missed the loving embrace and he would have missed the celebration. We miss those two important experiences when we fail to *celebrate* the sacrament of Penance. We deprive ourselves of actually being reunited with the community, and we deprive ourselves and the community of the opportunity to celebrate this reunion. There are indeed good reasons for celebrating the sacrament of Penance today.

CHAPTER 14

The sacrament of Penance – what do I say?

In working with parents, I often find that many of them have not celebrated the sacrament of Penance for a long time. One reason is that they are embarrassed because they simply don't know how to celebrate the sacrament today.

Actually, the Church offers three ways of celebrating the sacrament. The first rite of reconciliation is the Rite for Reconciliation of Individual Penitents. It has generally the same format that many people were used to previously in 'going to confession'. However, people now have the option either to confess to the priest face-to-face or to remain behind a screen or curtain.

In preparing children for First Confession I am amazed at how little trouble they have confessing face-to-face. To them it is perfectly normal. 'How else would you speak to someone?' they often ask. They feel very comfortable with their parish priests and would really not think of celebrating the sacrament any other way, unless their parents have advised them otherwise.

Adults usually have more difficulty because they were trained to confess behind a screen. There was some fear that if the priest recognised them, he would forever remember what great sinners they were. Would they ever be able to face the priest in another situation if he really knew what sinners they were?

First of all, a priest cannot possibly remember every confession, nor would he want to. Second, the role of the priest is to preach conversion to sinners. There would be no need to do so without some assumption that people are in need of conversion. Third, it is really difficult to remain totally anonymous. There are distinctive after-shaves and perfumes, as well as tone of voice and characteristic expressions. Even confessing in a whisper does not totally disguise the person. So there is really nothing to fear in confessing face-to-face.

The outward sign in the sacrament of Penance consists of two simultaneous gestures. The priest says the words of absolution while extending his hands in blessing. The extension of the hands is a healing gesture. If a person confesses behind a screen, he or she misses the richness and beauty of this symbolic act, unless the reconciliation room were designed like an incubator, which would allow the hands to protrude awkwardly through the screen!

One of the most refreshing aspects of the sacrament is the way it allows a person to see and feel more directly the love and compassion of the priest. Something reassuring is missed by remaining isolated behind a screen. But a person should not let concern over whether or not to celebrate the sacrament face-to-face discourage him or her from celebrating the sacrament. A person always has the option of celebrating either way. More important is the person's serious desire to celebrate conversion in his or her life.

You prepare for celebrating the sacrament by praying and reflecting on your life. The Gospels are valuable for stimulating this kind of reflection. What brought you to this moment? Was there a particular Gospel passage that moved you? How does your life relate to the Gospel, to what Jesus asks of you? You needn't worry about an exact numerical counting of sins, although the priest may ask approximately how many times something was done or not done, only to obtain a better understanding of the seriousness of the problem.

When you enter the reconciliation room, the priest will greet you either with a formal prayer or an informal welcome. If you are going face-to-face, you may be seated across from the priest.

The priest may ask whether you have reflected on a particular Scripture passage. If not, and that is all right, the priest may either read or have you read a short passage. Then the priest will ask for your confession.

After hearing your confession, the priest will talk to you about what you have said, provide counsel, and give encouragement for living a better life. The priest will then propose a penance, which is intended to help you make amends for your sins and also to help you change your life. Thus, the penance may not be limited to reciting prayers, but may involve performing some work of kindness or charity.

After assigning the penance the priest will ask you to say a prayer of sorrow or contrition. You may choose from a variety of optional formal prayers or express contrition in your own words. Often you will find formal prayers printed on a card that is kept in the reconciliation room.

Then the priest will extend his hands over you and pray the prayer of absolution. It is a beautiful prayer that you should listen carefully to:

> God, the Father of mercies,
> through the death and resurrection of his Son
> has reconciled the world to himself
> and sent the Holy Spirit among us
> for the forgiveness of sins;
> through the ministry of the Church
> may God give you pardon and peace,
> and I absolve you from your sins
> in the name of the Father, and of the Son,
> and of the Holy Spirit.

This prayer is a beautiful expression of the saving power of God in the Trinity continued through the ministry of the Church. It is not the priest who forgives our sins, because we are absolved in the name of the Father, Son and Holy Spirit. It is God who forgives our sins through the saving work continued in the Church.

The celebration of Penance concludes with a dismissal, expressed either formally or informally. Simple. Nothing really complicated about it. And if you aren't sure, the priest is there to help. No need to feel embarrassed.

Another way of celebrating the sacrament of Penance is called the Rite of Reconciliation of Several Penitents with Individual Confession and Absolution. In this rite people gather together in church for a celebration that at first resembles the beginning of a Mass. The rite usually includes a gathering hymn, introduction, opening prayers, and liturgy of the word, followed by a homily. After the homily there are opportunities for a general examination of conscience, confession of sin, and expression of sorrow. Then there is the opportunity for individual confessions.

However, the individual confessions in this rite take an abbreviated form because many of the prayers have already been prayed in community. They simply include the confession of sin and the acceptance of absolution and a penance.

When all of the confessions have been completed, everyone gathers for a prayer of thanksgiving, a blessing, dismissal, and concluding hymn.

A third way to celebrate the sacrament of Penance is the Rite for Reconciliation of Several Penitents with General Confession and Absolution. This rite is similar to the second except that it includes no individual confessions. Instead, all reflect on their sinfulness, acknowledge their sinfulness in a communal prayer, and receive forgiveness of their sins. However, serious sins must still be confessed individually at the first available opportunity.

This rite is to be used only when the number of penitents is so large that it would be impossible for a priest to adequately hear each confession. This rite is sometimes used, with the permission of the bishop, during Advent and Lent when large numbers of penitents usually come to celebrate the sacrament.

No matter which of the three rites is celebrated, the important aspects of the sacrament of Penance remain the same. The sacrament celebrates conversion, a change of heart in which a person recognises that his or her life needs to be re-directed toward God. It always includes confession, whether it be individual as in the first and second rites or communal as in the third rite, and the admission that a person's life needs changing. It always includes contrition, the expression of sorrow for what the person has done. It always includes absolution, which frees the person from that which has kept him or her in bondage. And finally, it always includes an act of penance, which both makes amends for sin and expresses the new direction that a person's life is taking.

Above all, the celebration of the sacrament of Penance should result in a joyful celebration! As Jesus said, 'there will be more joy in heaven over one sinner who repents than over ninety-nine righteous people who have no need of repentance' (Luke 15:7).

CHAPTER 15

What's happened to Confirmation?

I remember some aspects of my Confirmation very clearly, even though I was confirmed many years ago. The vividness of this memory is probably due in part to the intensity of my preparation in a Catholic school. I remember using a red paper-covered book that we studied dutifully, especially for purposes of memorising answers to questions in the back of the book. Our motivation for memorising each word was the fear that we would not be confirmed if the bishop were to ask us a question and we did not know the answer.

The bishop came to confirm every two or three years. Thus, two or three classes were confirmed at the same time. Our church could not accommodate the three hundred confirmands and three hundred sponsors, so Confirmation took place in the parish gym. Confirmands sat in the front of the gym and sponsors were perfectly aligned in the back. Everything was well synchronised so that the appropriate sponsor would be standing behind the correct confirmand at the moment of Confirmation. At least I think my sponsor was behind me at the time.

I remember the emphasis that was placed on our becoming 'soldiers of Christ' and receiving a slap on the cheek from the bishop to remind us of our willingness to stand up for Christ and suffer for him. I took a new name, Joseph. I remember standing in the rain after the service because I got separated from my sponsor.

I remember that no one asked me if I wanted to be confirmed. I was only told that I wouldn't be if I didn't know all the answers to the questions. Nobody has ever challenged my faith to the point of requiring me to die for my faith, and I have never used my Confirmation name in any legal document. I remember hearing over and over again that we would receive the gifts of the Holy Spirit at Confirmation. I got a new tennis racket and ten pounds. From the perspective of many years I often wish I had the opportunity to celebrate my Confirmation again.

Some things have changed in the celebration of Confirmation, but others have remained the same. Confirmation was and still is closely related to the sacrament of Baptism. I was told at the ripe old age of eleven that I would be able to do for myself in Confirmation what my parents had done for me when I was baptised as an infant – to accept the Catholic faith. But there is an even closer link between Baptism and Confirmation.

To understand something of this link, we need to examine the origins of Confirmation. In the early Church, as in the RCIA today, Baptism and Confirmation were celebrated at the same time. In fact, in the early Church, Baptism and Confirmation were so connected that they were seen as one sacrament, with Confirmation simply being the completion of the rite of Baptism. In time the rites became separated. Priests baptised infants, but bishops retained the right to confirm. As the Church spread, people moved farther and farther away from their bishops, and, thus, bishops had to 'ride the circuit', visiting a town or village only once every few years. When the bishop visited, he confirmed those who had been baptised as infants. Gradually, the sacrament of Confirmation emerged as a distinct sacrament. However, it is still seen today as a sacrament that completes Baptism.

Perhaps the words of anointing in Confirmation explain it best: '... be sealed with the Gift of the Holy Spirit.' The 'sealing' in the anointing shows that something is being completed. But what is completed? What was left incomplete?

In Baptism we become graced by God, we share in the life of God – Father, Son, and Holy Spirit. Because we are plunged into the death and resurrection of Christ in Baptism, we become adopted children of God. Baptism, then, is like our personal celebration of Easter. It is a sacrament of new life. But even for the apostles, the Easter experience was not sufficient to carry on the work of Christ. As tremendous an experience as it was, the apostles were still incomplete after the Easter event; that is, they were lacking the power of the Spirit. It wasn't until Pentecost that a dramatic change took place in the apostles. Only then did the presence of the Spirit empower them to go forth and witness their faith. Pentecost completes Easter

– rounds it out, so to speak. In a similar way, Confirmation completes Baptism. It seals our own Easter so that we can be empowered and be full disciples of Christ.

If Confirmation is seen as a sacrament of 'mission', of strengthening confirmands to go forth, then it makes sense to confirm adults immediately after their Baptism, as in the RCIA. But when do we confirm baptised infants? The age for celebrating the sacrament of Confirmation varies today because each bishop is allowed to determine the minimum age for his own diocese. However, most Confirmations take place during the later years of primary school. Perhaps no age is a good age, for when are we ever really ready to go out and witness the faith?

The emphasis on mission and witnessing the faith today is similar to the 'soldier of Christ' emphasis from the past. While today's emphasis is less militaristic and more peaceful, it is still full of the same responsibility to live out faithfully our commitment to Christ in the Church.

Where older children are being confirmed today, the preparation for Confirmation has changed as well. The preparation may well include a weekend retreat, which gives candidates the opportunity to seriously reflect on the meaning of their faith. Often candidates for Confirmation are required to complete a certain number of service hours or a special project. These projects are intended to help candidates understand the type of Christian lives that they should lead after Confirmation. The problem, though, is that many candidates see these projects as 'things to do' in order to 'get confirmed'.

The problem may not be with the projects but with how they are presented. How many parishes have follow-up programmes after Confirmation, programmes that continue to explain the meaning of Confirmation and in which parishioners continue to walk with the newly confirmed to help them live their faith? How many parishes have a retreat *after* Confirmation to help the confirmands reflect on the significance of what has happened to them? Imagine what might happen to our young people if parishes spent as much time and energy on post-Confirmation programmes as they do in preparing people for Confirmation! In many parishes, Confirmation remains the last formal contact that the parish has with its young people. Confirmation becomes equated with graduation. But that could change if parishes would be willing to support young people after Confirmation.

Another way that the connection between Baptism and Confirmation is seen today is in the selection of a sponsor for Confirmation. Candidates today are strongly encouraged to select their godparents as their sponsors for Confirmation. The selection of a sponsor should not be done lightly – just to repay a social favour, for instance. The sponsor should be one who truly witnesses the faith to the candidate and who can support the candidate before and after Confirmation. A person who is asked to be a sponsor should take it not only as a great honour, but also as a great responsibility to be a partner in the faith.

The selection of a new name for Confirmation was always an exciting moment. The new name was intended to show that a new person was affirming the faith. Often a young person selected the name of a saint whom he or she admired. However, the emphasis today is for the candidate to affirm his or her baptismal name as a sign of affirming his or her own Baptism.

Today Confirmations are generally celebrated within a Eucharistic Liturgy with the parish and family and friends gathered together. The celebration within a Eucharistic Liturgy helps show the connectedness among the sacraments of initiation – Baptism, Eucharist and Confirmation. Also, Confirmation is not a private affair. It is a celebration of God's continued presence in and by the whole Church. Confirmation is not just something a person 'gets'. Confirmation is an expression of the confirmand's commitment to live the Gospel as he or she is sent on the mission of the Church – the mission of Christ.

The usual administrator of the sacrament of Confirmation for those baptised as infants remains the bishop. However, in some dioceses bishops have appointed special priest administrators because of the great number of confirmands and because of the great distances separating parishes.

The sacrament of Confirmation has undergone many changes throughout history, and it will probably continue to experience changes. However, it remains a sacrament of the Holy Spirit that completes Baptism and strengthens us to go forth and witness the Gospel to all people.

CHAPTER 16

Marriage – is it still till death do us part?

It's a beautiful Saturday afternoon. The church is crowded with family and friends as a young couple come to celebrate their wedding. They are starry-eyed and radiant. They longingly gaze into each other's eyes and almost sigh as they profess to each other their unending love. Perhaps thousands of pounds were spent on all the details. Beautiful music, gorgeous gowns, blooming flowers, gold this, silver that. They leave the church to celebrate and to live happily ever after.

But not too many years down the road we hear that this couple is divorced – a more and more common story today. What has happened to the sacrament of Marriage? Isn't marriage till death do us part? What happens to couples who divorce? Has Church teaching on marriage changed? Does the Church permit divorce? What is an annulment?

Marriage is still a sacrament in the Catholic Church, and it is still viewed by the Church as an indissoluble bond. There is more to celebrating a marriage than conducting a beautiful wedding service. Marriage is a celebration of God's love expressed in the love between the bride and the groom.

The Church's understanding of the bond of marriage comes from Genesis: 'That is why a man leaves his father and mother and clings to his wife, and the two of them become one body' (Genesis 2:24). Jesus not only affirmed the sacredness of the bond of marriage but further stated, 'Therefore what God has joined together, no human being must separate' (Mark 10:9).

Jesus performed his first miracle, as recorded in John's Gospel, at a wedding feast in Cana. He turned water into wine in order to help the newly-weds avoid embarrassment. Perhaps he prevented their first marital row, as one spouse might have said to the other, 'I told you to order more wine!' Jesus wanted them to begin their life together in love and peace.

When Jesus spoke to the Samaritan woman at the well, he showed his attitude toward the sacredness of the marriage bond when he asked the woman to call her husband. The woman replied that she did not have a husband, and Jesus said, 'You are right in saying, "I do not have a husband." For you have had five husbands, and the one you have now is not your husband' (John 4:17-18).

Saint Paul wrote about the sacredness of marriage. While he is often criticised for being one-sided in stating that wives should be obedient to their husbands, he also states that husbands should love their wives as they love their own bodies (Ephesians 5:21-32). At the conclusion of his discourse Paul sees the relationship between a man and a woman in marriage as the type of relationship that Christ has to the Church (Ephesians 5:32). This is a relationship of total love, never-ending love.

The relationship between Christ and the Church is not based upon the idea of a contract but upon the biblical concept of covenant love. This concept developed gradually in the Hebrew Scriptures. Covenant love expressed God's total love for the Israelites. No matter what the Israelites did, no matter how seriously they sinned, God always forgave them and welcomed them back.

The new covenant finds its greatest expression of love in the Eucharist. In Eucharist Jesus gives himself totally, Body and Blood, for our salvation. Marriages should be based on this kind of covenant love!

Perhaps one of the reasons for the high divorce rate today is that too many couples approach marriage as a contract rather than as a covenant. In some countries the legal system has contributed to this contractual emphasis by attempting to protect both parties with prenuptial agreements 'just in case' of divorce. While legal protection has certainly helped protect the rights of people, perhaps too many couples approach marriage simply from this legalistic, contractual aspect of 'just in case' instead of celebrating Marriage as a sacrament.

Sacraments are neither 'things we do' nor are they 'things we get'. Sacraments are special encounters with God through the signs and symbols found in the Church. People cannot be forced to celebrate a sacrament. Sacraments must be celebrated freely. People must know what they are celebrating in a sacrament, and part of this means that people must be united to the Church in order to celebrate a sacrament. In Marriage, therefore, the couple must know that they are indeed celebrating a sacrament that is an expression of God's love. They must know that it is an indissoluble union, and that they cannot place any conditions upon the relationship. Married love is unconditional love.

Sometimes, however, even the seemingly best relationship, even the marriage that seemed to be 'made in heaven' may end in divorce. What happens to Catholics who divorce?

Marriage as a social institution is regulated by the civil laws of society. Thus, divorce is a civil termination of the legal agreement between the two spouses. The Church does not grant divorces. The Church celebrates a sacramental bond between two people. In the case of divorce, the Church still recognises that a sacramental bond exists for the couple. 'What God has joined together, no human being must separate.' Thus, divorced people who do not remarry are still able to fully participate in the sacramental life of the Church. They are not second-class citizens, but full members of the Church.

Even though the Church still recognises a sacramental union, it does not callously ignore the pain and suffering experienced in a broken relationship. Many dioceses and parishes provide support groups, weekend retreats, and other programmes to help divorced people deal with this experience. The Church continues the ministry of Jesus by ministering to people hurting at this time.

After a civil divorce, either party of a Catholic marriage may petition the Church for an annulment of the marriage. An annulment, or declaration of nullity, is not a divorce. Rather, it is a declaration by the Church that a sacramental union was not possible at the time of the marriage.

There are numerous reasons why a sacramental union may not have been possible. Perhaps there was some impediment to the marriage, such as inability to consummate the marriage, which either party did not know about or did not reveal prior to the marriage. Perhaps there was psychological immaturity, inability to understand the sacramental nature of Marriage or unwillingness to see the sacramental union as an indissoluble bond.

Cases for annulment usually begin with a parish priest who presents the petition to a diocesan tribunal or court. The process for judging whether or not a marriage is to be declared null is a time-consuming process, sometimes lasting more than a year. Although it may seem that many people receive declarations of nullity, the Church does not grant one in every case. Since the Church has the duty to preserve the bond of a valid marriage, it is very careful about declaring a marriage invalid. For these reasons, neither party in a marriage that has been terminated by civil laws and that has been presented for annulment is free to marry within the Church until a declaration of nullity is granted.

While ministering to those suffering from separation and divorce, the Church has also done much recently to help build and support loving relationships between couples. Marriage preparation programmes have attempted to facilitate open and honest communication between the couple before marriage so that the couple may continue to discuss important issues for the rest of their lives. Programmes for the engaged often consist of all-day sessions or even weekend retreats that give couples the opportunity to reflect on the seriousness and sacredness of the sacramental union.

Marriage Encounter and similar movements have provided great impetus for making good marriages even better. Related programmes, such as evenings for couples and Image Groups, help couples continue the spirit of love enkindled on a weekend encounter.

Many parishes and dioceses offer continuing programmes for marriage enrichment. They feature speakers and small group discussions that can support people in their marriages. And if such programmes are not available in parishes, there are many community and social organisations that offer a variety of services to strengthen and support marriage relationships.

Marriage is still a sacred union in the Catholic Church. Good marriages are more than carefully-planned, elaborate wedding ceremonies. Good marriages require a great deal of love and hard work. They require good communication and the total gift of self, the way Christ has given himself to all of us. As Jesus said, '… love one another as I love you. No one has greater love than this, to lay down one's life for one's friends' (John 15:12-13). Certainly one would hope that spouses would be 'best friends' to each other. Therefore, their love, their marriage should be a covenant, in which they love each other just as God has loved all of us.

CHAPTER 17

What's happening to the priesthood?

When I was in the early years of a Catholic elementary school, it seemed that an equal number of boys wanted to be firemen, policemen and priests when they grew up. I myself was impressed with the seemingly ideal life of a priest. I remember the pastor driving a big maroon car, smoking an occasional cigar and walking peacefully around the parish grounds while praying his breviary. Everyone seemed to respect him. He always sat at the head table and was always called upon to lead the prayer and to say a few words to the people. What a life, I thought.

When I entered the seminary in my first year of high school, we were in a new building. Almost two hundred were in my class. Four years later seventy-two of us remained to graduate. Twelve from that class were eventually ordained. Today, more than twenty-five years later, the secondary school seminary is closed and the college has moved to a nearby Catholic university. Where have all the vocations to the priesthood gone, and what's happening to the priesthood?

I entered the seminary just as Vatican II was beginning. The image of the priest at that time resembled the characters portrayed by Barry Fitzgerald and Bing Crosby in *The Bells of St Mary's* and *Going My Way*. A much different style and image of priesthood is emerging today.

While style and image may be changing, some things remain the same. Ordination to the priesthood is a sacrament of the Catholic Church. Deacons, priests and bishops all receive the sacrament of Holy Orders.

Transitional deacons are ordained about one year prior to their ordination to the priesthood. For them, the diaconate becomes one of the steps to the priesthood. Permanent deacons are ordained for life. The permanent diaconate was restored in the Catholic Church after Vatican II. Permanent deacons serve the Church voluntarily and must, therefore, have other means of supporting themselves. Permanent deacons may be married at the time of ordination. However, those who are unmarried take a vow of celibacy.

Following the tradition of the first deacons of the Church, permanent deacons often minister to the widowed, sick, homebound, and the poor. However, they may minister in other areas as well. Deacons can baptise, distribute Communion, witness marriages, proclaim the Gospel and preach, and conduct benedictions, wakes and committals at burials.

Deacons are not mini-priests. They serve the Church in their own proper capacity as ordained ministers.

In ordination to the priesthood a man is set apart by and for the community to be their spiritual leader, to model a spiritual life and to show what it means to live the Gospel. Priests are given authority to baptise, preside at the Eucharistic celebration, hear confessions and forgive sins, anoint the sick, witness marriages and, in some cases, confirm. Because of their role as spiritual leaders, priests have traditionally been given the title, 'Father' by Catholics.

In ordination to the episcopacy a priest becomes a bishop. A bishop shares in the apostolic succession and governs a large geographical area called a diocese. A bishop is an administrator of all of the sacraments. Thus, only a bishop may ordain deacons, priests and other bishops.

Jesus did not leave the Church a blueprint for the diaconate, priesthood and episcopacy. In fact, Jesus never referred to his apostles as priests or bishops. There was no ordination ceremony such as we are accustomed to celebrating today. The institution of the sacrament of Holy Orders is generally seen to have taken place at the Last Supper. In John's account, Jesus washes the feet of his apostles, a task usually left to household servants and slaves. Yet, Jesus told his disciples, 'I have given you a model to follow, so that as I have done for you, you should also do' (John 13:15).

Priesthood, therefore, involves more than presiding at Eucharistic Liturgy and administrating the sacraments. It means washing feet. The priesthood involves a life of total dedication and service. The practical application of that challenge continues to influence our understanding of priesthood today.

The role of the Jewish priesthood influenced the early Christian understanding of priest. The role of the priest was to offer sacrifice. In the Letter to the Hebrews Jesus is seen as the great high priest who offered himself up for our sins. As the early Christians began to see the Eucharist as more than just a meal – as a sacrificial meal – the presider at that meal was seen as one who offered sacrifice, that is, a priest.

While priests in the Christian tradition have always had a spiritual leadership function, priests have also assumed many other responsibilities. For example, a priest is often seen not only as a spiritual counsellor but also as a psychological counsellor. But, since more advanced training is required in this field, today many priests wisely refer some people who need psychological counselling to professionals better prepared to help them.

The complexity of the modern parish requires skills in administration, management and financial planning that were not necessary only a few years ago. These duties are not integral to priesthood, and many priests wisely use the resources of parishioners who have expertise in these areas.

The changing understanding of the role of the priest may be caused in part by the changing understanding of the role of the laity. In the past it seemed that only a priest could lead the prayer at a meeting and that the pastor's presence was necessary at every parish function as a sort of sanction of the event. But lay people have discovered that they can lead prayer and that a priest does not need to be present for every parish activity.

As spiritual leaders, priests have a major responsibility to help their parishioners understand the relatedness between hearing the Gospel and living the Gospel each day, between celebrating the Eucharist and being Eucharist to the world. For many priests today this means being actively involved in the world, taking stands on justice issues and ministering to those who are outcasts. While some people are disturbed by this involvement in secular affairs, others find in this involvement examples of how they are truly to live the Gospel.

It has been a tradition in the Catholic Church that only males may be ordained. Why can't women be ordained? While it may appear that the Church is lagging in providing for equality, women's rights is a relatively modern phenomenon. Governments did not even grant women the right to vote until 1920.

Change comes slowly, especially in the universal Church, which must consider the needs and sensitivities of people all over the world. But as women begin to assume their rightful places in world affairs, perhaps the Church will more seriously examine the role of women in spiritual leadership positions and ordained ministries.

It has also been a discipline in the Western Roman Catholic Church that priests take a vow of celibacy. Will that ever change? The discipline of celibacy wasn't required until around the tenth century. Certainly there are advantages to a celibate life, especially in a life of dedicated service. But celibacy is not integral to priesthood, and we could have the return of a married clergy at some point in the future.

Would permitting a married clergy increase vocations to the priesthood? Perhaps for a short time those presently not responding to the call of priesthood because it requires celibacy might seek ordination. But the long-term effect is uncertain. Even religions that permit ministers to marry are experiencing shortages of people responding to the ministry.

What can we do to help remedy the present shortage of vocations to the priesthood? We can certainly continue to pray that young men will respond to the call to serve as priests. We can also pray that our present priests will be dedicated servants who will serve as viable role models for those contemplating priesthood. Perhaps we can simply be less critical and more supportive of our priests. It is often easy to be negative and to complain, especially when we may not like what a priest says or does. Yet, our young children and youth hear our negative comments, and that certainly does not encourage them to think about priesthood as a vocation. Prayer and positive words and actions will go a long way in helping our priests serve as Jesus wants them to.

CHAPTER 18

Who's running the parish?

At the parish level today, more and more lay people are actively involved in leadership positions through formal ministries and especially in such areas as the parish council. In some parishes it seems as if the council runs the parish and the parish priest has little to say. In other parishes the parish council and lay people in general have little impact because the parish priest refuses to listen to anyone. But there are also many instances in which priest and parish council work together effectively.

It is difficult sometimes to understand the leadership and authority structure of the Church today. What leadership roles and authority do lay people have in a parish? Who's running the parish?

People who live in democratic countries, in particular, have a problem in trying to understand the governing structure of the Catholic Church. We sometimes tend to compare the Church structure with our own civil governmental structure. But the Catholic Church is not a democracy. We Catholics do not elect our bishops or parish priests. We do not operate by the principle of one person, one vote.

This problem in understanding the authority structure of the Catholic Church has developed in part because the Second Vatican Council placed tremendous emphasis on the idea that we are the Church, each and every one of us. Thus, in the minds of some, if we are the Church, then we should make decisions about Church governance. But the bishops of Vatican II were not speaking about government in calling us the Church. They were speaking about our spiritual union together in Christ.

In one sense, what the bishops said seemed revolutionary because for a long time in Church history the Church was equated mainly with its hierarchical structure. This structure resembles a pyramid: pope at the top, followed by bishops and priests, and, finally, lay people at the bottom. But Saint Paul wrote, '... so we, though many, are one body in Christ...' (Romans 12:5). And Jesus himself said, 'For where two or three are gathered together in my name, there am I in the midst of them' (Matthew 18:20). Thus, the Church is present wherever two or three gather in the name of Jesus.

Saint Agnes Parish in the inner city is the Church just as much as Saint Philip's Parish in a rural community is the Church. These are not subdivisions or franchises of the Church. Each is the Church totally present in these locations. These communities have been recognised by the bishop as groups who gather in the name of Jesus, who celebrate the sacraments and who proclaim and live the Good News. Each parish is the Church totally present in a given locality or for a designated group of people.

But aren't there many Churches, then? No, there is only one Church, for the Church is the Body of Christ and there can be only one Christ. But that body is totally and really present wherever two or more gather in Jesus' name, wherever the sacraments are celebrated and the Gospel is preached.

There is no other body or group with which the Church can be adequately compared. But despite the limitations of comparison, it might be helpful to compare the Church with a world organisation such as the Red Cross. The symbol of a red cross is a universal symbol, easily identifiable and understood by anyone in the world. The sign of a red cross represents emergency care in time of disaster. The symbol is generally respected. In time of war, buildings displaying the red cross are known to be hospitals or shelters and are not to be bombed. People wearing the red cross are known to be unarmed and are not to be attacked.

As an organisation, the Red Cross is not just its executive board. The Red Cross is not just its paid leaders in any level of management. The Red Cross exists wherever people join together as *bona fide* members of the organisation. The Red Cross is just as totally present to the families of a burned-out apartment complex in New York as it is to the survivors of a flood in India. Isn't there only one Red Cross? Yes. But wherever there are people in need, the Red Cross is totally present to them.

But the Red Cross is a human organisation that needs managing. Thus, it is divided into national groups, regions, and local chapters.

For management purposes, for ease in administration, the Red Cross needs to divide itself into these smaller units. But the Red Cross is just as present in a local blood drive as it is in a national fund-raising campaign. The Red Cross is not just management but also the volunteers who care and respond.

In a similar way, the Church needs to be divided into smaller units for administrative purposes. The universal Church is thus divided into dioceses and parishes, but each truly and totally represents the whole Church.

Most Catholics understand the meaning of Church through their experience of Church at the parish level. A parish is usually a geographic designation with territorial boundaries. The parish is thus the Church present to all people in a specific area. There are also, of course, parishes which are not geographical areas but specific groups of people, like the Travellers in Ireland.

The parish priest, appointed by the bishop, is the official head of a parish. However, in some cases, especially where there is a shortage of priests, like in some dioceses in America, one priest may serve two or more parishes, or a layman appointed by the bishop may administrate the parish.

Parishioners have no choice in the selection of their parish priest. However, in some dioceses, parishioners may be consulted about the type of pastor they think would be best suited to their parish. But it is only a consultation. The bishop makes the final decision.

Many parishes today have a parish pastoral council or at least a finance and management council. The council is composed of the parish priest and several lay people elected or discerned to serve on the council. Usually one of the lay members serves as chairperson of the council meetings, but the parish priest is president of the council and has full veto power over its actions.

The council is an advisory body that determines parish needs and shapes policies to respond to those needs. For a parish management council, an example of a policy is the parish budget. The budget represents the allocation of parish money for specific needs. The council may have to examine, for instance, whether or not there should be a parish school. If so, then allocating money for the accomplishment of that initiative is shaping a policy. A parish may determine a need for responding to the poor through an outreach programme. Allocating money to support that vision thus becomes the shaping of a policy. And so on. Policies ultimately are subject to the approval of the parish priest, and it is the responsibility of the priest, as the administrator of the parish, to implement the approved policies.

A parish pastoral council often has committees that focus on the major areas of parish life: Liturgy, Christian formation, and the like. The committees are responsible for listening to the parishioners, prioritising needs, and developing a vision that is consistent with the total mission of the parish in order to meet those needs. Committees make recommendations to the council, which must bring all the needs together and re-prioritise them in light of the total mission of the parish. While a parish priest may not approve everything a council recommends, healthy dialogue between the priest and council will keep communication flowing and make for a vibrant and healthy parish.

While parish priests are ultimately responsible for the spiritual well-being of their parishioners, they cannot possibly listen to the concerns and needs of every parishioner on every aspect of parish life. Thus, parishioners should use the structures available to bring their concerns to the person or group designated to respond to those needs.

An organisational principle called *subsidiarity* applies to the Church. It means that nothing should be done at a higher level of the organisation that can be done at a lower level. If, for example, an exit light is burned out in church, there is no need to present the matter to the parish council or the property and maintenance committee when a simple note to the janitor would suffice. Thus, parishioners who wish to effect change should always begin at the lowest possible level of authority, with the person immediately in charge.

Jesus talked about this principle when he talked about the need for correcting someone:

> If your brother sins [against you], go and tell him his fault between you and him alone. If he listens to you, you have won over your brother. If he does not listen, take one or two others along with you, so that every fact may be established on the testi-

mony of two or three witnesses. If he refuses to listen to them, tell
the Church (Matthew 18:15-17).

In short, Jesus tells us to begin at the lowest level of authority, with
the person responsible for the action. The resolution of problems
and the creation of visions would probably go more smoothly if
more parishioners followed this process.

Yes, the parish priest is in charge of the parish, but each of us is a
member of the Church, the Body of Christ. As Saint Paul says:

> So then you are no longer strangers and sojourners, but you are
> fellow citizens with the holy ones and members of the household
> of God, built upon the foundation of the apostles and prophets,
> with Christ Jesus himself as the capstone. Through him the
> whole structure is held together and grows into a temple sacred
> in the Lord; in him you also are being built together into a dwell-
> ing place of God in the Spirit (Ephesians 2:19-22).

CHAPTER 19

What is lay ministry?

Until recently terms like minister and ministry were generally used by Catholics to describe non-Catholic religious leaders and activities. For instance, the pastor of the Protestant church down the block was a minister, not a priest. Television evangelists would exhort people to give donations toward their ministry. But Catholics today are becoming increasingly familiar with applying the words ministry and minister to Catholic activities, especially when these words refer to the service of lay people. What is lay ministry? And who is involved in it in the Catholic Church?

The root meaning of ministry is 'to serve'. All Christians, through Baptism, are called to minister or to serve: '... serve one another through love' (Galatians 5:13).

However, in its technical sense, minister has come to designate someone formally recognised to act on behalf of the Church in a specific ministry or area of service. For instance, all baptised people are called to respond to Jesus' command to visit the sick. We usually visit the sick out of friendship or love, most often because we know the person who is sick. But even when we visit strangers out of love, we rarely consider ourselves representatives of the faith community.

While the entire Church has a responsibility for visiting the sick, it would be impossible and impractical for hundreds of people from a parish to visit a parishioner who is ill. Thus, the Church designates individuals to represent the Church in visiting the sick. Often these people are designated to bring the Eucharist to the sick on a regular basis. These people are formally recognised as ministers and may be referred to as Ministers to the Sick, Ministers to the Homebound, Eucharistic Ministers to the Sick, or some similar term.

When members of a parish are designated as ministers, they are often commissioned in a special ceremony, usually as part of a Sunday Eucharistic Liturgy. The rest of the faith community should be grateful for the work of these people and support them in any way possible. However, it should be noted that the designation of some people as ministers does not in any way diminish the responsibility each person has to live the Gospel. All are called to be servants, that is, ministers.

There is no exact listing of the types of service that are officially recognised by the Church as lay ministries. However, to be recognised as lay ministry, an activity should continue the mission of the Church, which is the mission of Christ. Thus, the Church recognises the liturgical ministries that continue the praying and worshipping mission of the Church. Among the more commonly recognised liturgical ministries are those of the Minister of Hospitality, or Usher, Minister of the Word, or Lector, Eucharistic Minister, Minister of Song and Music, and Acolyte, or Server.

Another important area of recognised ministries in the Church is that of teaching. Thus, catechetical ministers are recognised as performing special service in the Church. Catechists and all those in similar positions should take their ministry seriously, realising that they are proclaiming the Gospel and helping others understand it.

Ministry should not be a response to arm twisting. It should be a loving response to the Lord's call.

Ministry also involves a careful deliberation or prayerful discernment of one's personal giftedness. In his letter to the Romans, Saint Paul writes about the use of our gifts:

> Since we have gifts that differ according to the grace given to us, let us exercise them: if prophecy, in proportion to the faith; if ministry, in ministering; if one is a teacher, in teaching; if one exhorts, in exhortation; if one contributes, in generosity; if one is over others, with diligence; if one does acts of mercy, with cheerfulness (Romans 12:6-8).

Paul also lists some ministries in order of their priority:

> Some people God has designated in the church to be, first, apostles; second, prophets; third, teachers; then, mighty deeds; then gifts of healing, assistance, administration, and varieties of tongues (1 Corinthians 12:28).

But no matter which gift a person has, or how the gift is ranked, a Christian serves because of love.

Although the shortage of priests may have helped us think more about lay ministries, the development of lay ministries today is not in response to the priest shortage. Rather, in developing lay ministries, we are returning to the spirit of the early Church in which the giftedness of each person was recognised and used. The beginning of preparation for lay ministry is discerning each person's giftedness. We should ask what special abilities and talents God has given us. Then we need to ask where God is calling us to use these gifts and with whom they are to be shared. When we reflect on God's call and on our giftedness, we might be led to places we had not ever thought about and find ourselves serving God in new and exciting ways.

Although some ministries are more sophisticated than others – requiring special training, skills and competencies – there are some characteristics that are common to all who minister. Among these characteristics is a deep faith life in which the minister is fully committed to Christ and the Catholic Church. A minister should view ministry as a response to the Lord's call, as a way of living out the baptismal commitment. In order to hear the Lord's call, a minister should be a person of prayer. And a minister's whole life should be filled with God's love so that the minister does not give scandal to others.

In other words, the minister's total life should witness the saving love and presence of God. But no less is really expected of all Christians, whether or not they are formally recognised ministers.

Some designated ministries, such as those of the priest and bishop, require full-time work. Lay people also serve in full-time ministries, such as directing religious education programmes, ministering to youth and young adults, directing adult and family formation programmes, serving as liturgical and music ministers or serving in a variety of other pastoral positions. In order to serve in these positions, a person usually has to have specialised training and education. The minimum educational requirement for these ministries is a university education.

Thus, a question sometimes arises regarding the compatibility of ministry with employment. Can a person be paid for ministering, for being of service? Jesus seems to have answered the question when he sent out his disciples and told them to carry nothing with them, for 'The labourer deserves his keep' (Matthew 10:10). Thus, if the Church demands educational preparation, with a person spending years getting an education, it seems only reasonable that the Church should compensate a person for that education and for the skills he or she brings to the ministry. So being an employed minister is not incompatible with being a servant.

There are many who serve the Church without being formally designated as ministers. There are those who serve meals to the homeless, those who count the money from the collections, those who decorate the church, set up tables for bingo, staple flyers into bulletins, keep the church cleaned. The list could go on and on. Even if these services are not formally recognised as ministries, those involved should know that they are indeed serving the Lord in the Church. Whatever they do contributes to building the kingdom of God.

The Church will probably struggle for some time with what is and what is not a designated lay ministry. And ministries will probably come and go as the needs of the Church change. But in whatever way we serve, however we minister, we should always 'serve the Lord with gladness' (Psalm 100:2).

CHAPTER 20

God, our Father – and our Mother?

One of the most vivid personal encounters with God was Moses' encounter with the burning bush. When Moses asked God's name, God replied, 'I am who am' (Exodus 3:14). This expression is the source of the word, *Yahweh*. 'I am who am' seems like an evasive answer. It does not provide us with the kind of proper name we are accustomed to hearing. Yet, 'I am who am' seems to imply everything there is to know about God: 'I am who I have been, am now, and who I will be forever.' The expression attempts to reveal as much about God as possible, without limiting God to a particular name, activity or description.

The Hebrews understood names differently from how we do. For the Hebrews, to name someone or something meant to have power over it. In the creation story Adam names the animals. This shows that humans have control over nature, that people are superior to animals. Therefore, naming God would be unthinkable to the Hebrews, for that would mean having power over God. God is God. God cannot be named by people.

The name *Yahweh* was considered so sacred that in later Jewish history it was replaced with the title *Adonai*, which meant 'Lord.' The Jews revered the name of God so much that they did not even want to pronounce it.

Is there any term or name that can adequately be used to address God or refer to God? Any word or image we use to designate or describe God is limiting. To call God Creator, for instance, describes only one activity of God. To refer to God as Merciful Judge or Almighty One also limits other possibilities. If we limit ourselves to only one title or designation, then we cheat ourselves of the richness of other expressions that can help us know and understand God better. Different images of God are presented in the Scriptures. In verse five of Psalm 121, God is called a 'guardian' and a 'shade'.

In verse one of Psalm 28, God is compared to a rock. Isaiah compares God to a shepherd.

Like a shepherd he feeds his flock;
in his arms he gathers the lambs,
Carrying them in his bosom,
and leading the ewes with care (Isaiah 40:11).

Each image attempts to describe some aspect of God to an individual or group in a particular situation. But God is not a sentinel, shepherd or midwife. God is not a rock or an eagle or any other image. Isaiah asks:

To whom can you liken God?
With what equal can you confront him? (Isaiah 40:18).

There is nothing we can liken God to. God is God.

There has been some concern recently about the language we use to describe God. Some find it too limiting to speak of God exclusively in male images because these fail to express the equally beautiful female images of God. In an age concerned about the rights and dignity of all people, it seems unjust to draw our images of God from only one half of the population. Others find feminine images of God offensive and almost blasphemous because our tradition has presented us with an almost exclusively masculine image of God. Should we be inclusive in our language about God? Is it possible to move beyond predominantly male images?

It is easy to understand why the Scriptures are filled with male images of God. Jewish society and culture, which developed our concepts of God, were male-dominated. Men were in power while women were generally subservient. Thus, God was depicted as male.

But even the author of the first creation story in Genesis seems to struggle with clearly identifying God:

Then God said:
'Let *us* make *man* in *our image*, after our likeness.
Let *them* have dominion over the fish ... and all the creatures
that crawl on the ground.'
God created *man* in *his image*;
in the *divine image* he created him;
male and *female* he created *them* (Genesis 1:26-27).

In looking at the emphasised words (emphasis is mine), we can get some sense of the possible attempt at inclusiveness: at including both masculine and feminine qualities in the image of God. Most Scripture scholars today agree that *humanity* is created in the image and likeness of God. Thus, the image of God includes both feminine and masculine aspects.

God was never revealed as only male. The God revealed to Moses, Yahweh, was neither male nor female: 'I am who am.' God is God. All we can do is use human images to attempt to describe the characteristics of God. If God is a warrior, it is because God was so described by a warring nation that saw the saving power and victory of God. If God is a king, it is because a nation gave God their total allegiance. If God is a shepherd, it is because of a people who understood and saw in God the best qualities of one who cares for the flocks.

Jesus referred to God as his loving Father. But Jesus could also have used female images to speak about God. However, these would probably not have been readily accepted and would only have detracted from Jesus' more important message. The issue of God's gender was not important at that time.

A problem that concerns many people today may have also existed at the time of Christ: The image of father is negative or meaningless to those who have been abandoned or abused by their natural fathers. Catechists often find this true when attempting to use the image of God as Father for the children they teach. For some people, to limit the image of God to one gender is to limit their possibility of coming to know and love God.

While the Gospels have Jesus identifying God as Father, what Jesus presents are beautiful images of God that could be images of a masculine or feminine parent. The image of a warm, loving and forgiving father as presented in the story of the prodigal child could just as easily be an image of a warm, loving and forgiving mother. Either image could express our understanding of God.

We may be jolted in our imaging of God when someone begins the Lord's Prayer by saying, 'Our Mother'. If this is done insensitively and without fully preparing people for understanding the totality of God, then such a change serves little purpose. Our change in images should be done out of love, to help others image the fullness and beauty of God.

It is wrong to attempt to correct one injustice with another injustice.

Imaging God as Mother is not totally wrong just as imaging God as Father is not totally correct. God is God, neither male nor female. In God there is the fullness of both feminine and masculine. All the beauty of creation is held within God. Saint John really puts it simply and best when he says, 'God is love' (1 John 4:8).

Therefore, we should feel free to address and understand God in whatever way we feel comfortable with and in whatever way helps us come to understand and love God better.

Slow steps are being taken to make our language inclusive, that is, to have our language include everyone. However, the English language does not have a personal pronoun that combines the feminine and masculine in a singular form. Thus, instead of using she or he and him or her to refer to God, we often have to re-arrange our sentence structure to avoid using pronouns. This can sometimes make for awkwardness of expression. However, some attempts are being made in this regard in our Scripture translations, in our liturgical prayers, and in our religious music.

Another area in which the Church is attempting to make its language inclusive is in its references to the people of God, to all people. It has been common for the Scriptures and Church writings to almost exclusively refer to 'men' or 'man' when all people are intended. But progress is being made. For example, the most recent translation of the New American Bible tells us: 'There is neither Jew nor Greek, there is neither slave nor free person, there is not male and female; for you are all one in Christ Jesus' (Galatians 3:28). It is interesting to note that the previous translation of the New American Bible stated: 'There does not exist among you Jew or Greek, slave or *freeman*....' (Emphasis is mine.)

Jesus is the fullest expression of God's love. To know Jesus is to know God. Therefore, we should not let any barrier exist to our understanding of that love. As Paul wrote:

> For I am convinced that neither death, nor life, nor angels, nor principalities, nor present things, nor future things, nor powers, nor height, nor depth, nor any other creature will be able to

separate us from the love of God in Christ Jesus our Lord (Romans 8:38-39).

To this list Paul may just as well have added 'language', for that should not keep us from the love of God either.

CHAPTER 21

Has Jesus become too human?

When I was in primary school, I was taught by nuns who wore full habits – floor-length black dresses and long, wide veils that covered everything on and around their heads. Under the veils they wore white hoods that pressed tightly against their heads and covered their ears. I always wondered how they could hear, but they seemed to have no difficulty detecting even the slightest whisper among students. There was a mystique about these women. Did they have hair? Did they really have ears? Did they even have legs? Nuns seemed so different from other people. Did they ever laugh or cry? Did they ever sleep? Did they sleep in their habits?

When nuns gradually changed to civilian garb, we became more aware of their human side. Yes, they did have hair, and they had ears and legs. Now, we became aware that they even laughed and cried, a fact which we may not have noticed before. We realised that there was a human side to nuns. They were indeed like the rest of us.

For a while we were almost overly attentive to the novelty of their human side. Sister Paschal Candle became Sister Susan, and she drove a car and did her shopping at the supermarket. For a brief historical moment many people became so preoccupied with the newness of the life-style of the nuns that they almost lost sight of the beauty of these women, of their tremendous love and dedication to their ministries.

Something similar has happened in our understanding of Jesus. We have removed the veil, so to speak, and have recently come to see a more human side to Jesus. Perhaps at this historical moment, we are too preoccupied with this physical side.

Throughout the history of the Catholic Church there have been theological shifts as the pendulum has moved from a concern with the human Jesus to a concern with the divine Jesus. As a matter of fact, during the first three hundred years of the Church's existence there was considerable debate about the identity of Jesus. Was Jesus totally divine and not human at all? Was Jesus totally human, someone who just seemed to be a super-person, but not divine? Was Jesus half-human and half-divine? The answers came in the formulation of the Nicene Creed, the creed which is commonly used in our Sunday Eucharistic Liturgies. Jesus is true God and true man. He is one person, the second person of the Trinity, with two natures, divine and human.

Looking at the total Jesus is like looking at an object through binoculars. Both lenses are needed to clearly see the correct image. If we close one eye, our image shifts to the other side. Imagine that one lens of the binoculars is the divine side of Jesus and the other is the human side. To close one eye gives us a distorted image of the total Jesus.

While it is difficult to find the precise reason for the recent shift in emphasis to the human side of Jesus, one possible explanation might be the renewed interest in the Scriptures. Recent biblical scholarship has attempted to place Jesus in a cultural and historical context, especially in attempting to explain the meaning of his teaching and ministry. Thus, for instance, we have come to a deep appreciation and understanding of the parables in seeing these as illustrations used by Jesus the rabbi, the teacher.

As we enter more deeply into the Scriptures, we are no longer afraid to realise that Jesus ate, slept, cried and laughed. For a long time these human acts seemed almost unbecoming of God. But we must realise that while Jesus is God, he is also human.

We have come to realise that the familiar portrayal of Jesus in Western European art is incorrect, even though we have done little to change this image. Jesus was a Jew, born of a Jewish mother, and he had all the physical characteristics of a Jewish person living two thousand years ago in Palestine. While recent artistic renditions of Jesus have not caught up with the truth that Jesus was indeed a Jew who was probably more dark-skinned than he is shown in our representations, some depictions are refreshing. Today Jesus is sometimes seen as a carpenter or as a smiling Jesus or even as a laughing Jesus who has just heard a really good joke.

Jesus was the son of a carpenter and probably worked as a carpenter until he began his public ministry. His hands were probably calloused and hurt from having splinters and slivers stuck in them. His lungs were probably filled with sawdust. Jesus probably didn't mind getting his hands dirty.

In plays and films such as *Jesus Christ Superstar* and *Godspell*, the human side of Jesus is vividly portrayed. Some people find these portrayals disturbing and almost blasphemous, while others are moved to greater faith because of them. But these portrayals are not new because the human side of Jesus has been written about many times throughout history.

One of the values in seeing a human side to Jesus is that it helps many people identify with him. Truly our brother, Jesus, as one of us, knew what it was like to put in a hard day's work. He knew what it was like to live in poverty and be oppressed. He felt hunger and he experienced joy and sadness. He was compassionate and responded lovingly to the needs of others. But he also got angry. He hated sin but loved the sinner. He was like us in all things except sin.

When Jesus told us how to live, he did not talk 'off the top of his head'. As one of us, he shared our humanity and lived the same struggles as we do. Jesus did not just tell us how to live. He showed us by living life to the fullest. And he showed us that the ultimate goal in life is to love, even if that means we might have to die.

But there's more to Jesus than just a human being who lived life to the fullest. Jesus is truly God. As the centurion professed when Jesus died, 'Truly this man was the Son of God!' (Mark 15:39).

Sometimes we dismiss what Jesus did and the problems he had because we think that Jesus could turn on the divine side when the going got tough. But Jesus' divinity wasn't some sort of magical safety valve that he could use to rescue himself. Jesus showed us one human characteristic that we often fail to live up to – obedience. Obedience even unto the cross. Jesus was probably just as afraid of death as anyone else is. When he encountered death, he prayed, 'Father, if you are willing, take this cup away from me' (Luke 22:42). But then he also added, '... still, not my will but yours be done' (Luke 22:42). To be fully human is to do God's will.

We need to keep both lenses focused as we look at Jesus so that we can get the total picture. But for the present, we should consider ourselves fortunate to have an opportunity to gaze upon the human side a little more intensely.

I recently returned to my Catholic primary school for a meeting. Walking down the hall, I encountered the nun who had taught me music when I was a student there many years ago. She was still teaching music, but she looked different. She no longer wore the full habit and veil. When I saw her, I instinctively reached out and we embraced, human to human. We met as friends. I had no less respect for her as a vowed religious and for all that she does to serve the Lord just because she was wearing a skirt and blouse rather than a habit.

In the same way, we have an opportunity for a more personal encounter with the human Jesus. Sometimes it seems as if we have been able to bridge two thousand years of history and actually 'be there' with Jesus. The encounter with the human side helps us, I hope, to encounter and understand something of the divine side, the saving Lord of history, Jesus, the Son of God.

Have we over-emphasised the human side of Jesus? Only history might be able to answer that question. But so long as we keep a balance, so long as we keep focused on the total person of Jesus Christ, then the encounter with the human Jesus can be a deeply moving spiritual experience, and we should be happy for the opportunity to experience Jesus in this way.

CHAPTER 22

Is there still a place for honouring Mary?

What did the Second Vatican Council tell us about Mary? Many people who had grown up with special Marian devotions felt that the council did not give Mary adequate attention. Some people felt that the Second Vatican Council ended the role of Mary as we once knew and revered her. None of the sixteen documents of Vatican II is devoted to Mary. The bishops themselves argued about where they should speak of Mary. They finally agreed that their statement on Mary should not stand alone but should be included in their most important document, the *Dogmatic Constitution on the Church*. Chapter VIII in this document speaks about Mary and shows the importance of Mary for the Church. The bishops set the stage for Mary being designated as the Mother of the Church. This is only logical because if the Church is the Body of Christ and Mary is the Mother of Christ, then Mary is certainly the Mother of the Church. This may not sound revolutionary, but perhaps we have never before seriously considered her in this role.

The Second Vatican Council was a council about the Church. Thus, it was only appropriate that the council should consider Mary in relationship to the Church. It is indeed an honour for Mary to be so considered, and as we uncover the richness of meaning in what the fathers of the council said, we will come to honour Mary in new and meaningful ways.

Mary, Mother of the Church. What does that mean for us?

Children often reflect the values and behaviour of their parents. If we want to understand a child, we often need only to know the parents. How does Mary, as our Mother, want us to act? By turning to Mary as the Mother of the Church – our Mother – we should be able to find out something about how we are to behave.

Mary does not stand in the way of salvation, nor do we gain salvation through Mary. Salvation is gained only through Jesus Christ. This is something we must always remember in our devotion to Mary because it is something that is sometimes confusing to those outside the Catholic community. Perhaps the best example of Mary's role in the Church is found in the story of the wedding at Cana. Mary tells the servants, 'Do whatever he tells you' (John 2:5). Those words might as well have been addressed to all of us, for that is what Mary as our Mother really directs us to do: 'Do whatever he tells you.' Mary helps us focus our attention on her Son.

It is interesting to note that while Mary is the Mother of the Church, she is also the first member of that Church. We are joined to Mary in her humanity. Mary was in need of salvation just as we are, even though she was born without original sin. Mary had to make her *fiat*, say her yes to God, just as we do. Mary could not have been saved had it not been for the death and resurrection of her Son.

Mary was the first evangeliser when she brought the Good News to her cousin, Elizabeth. The role of the Church is primarily to evangelise, to bring the Good News of salvation to all people. Thus, we can turn to Mary and see how this is to be done.

Mary exemplifies obedience: 'May it be done to me according to your word' (Luke 1:38). Even in the seemingly strangest of situations, even without fully understanding what was to happen or how it would happen, Mary was obedient because of her faith in God. This is an example for her child, the Church. We should be obedient even when we do not fully understand what is happening. Like Mary, the Church should be 'the handmaid of the Lord' (Luke 1:38).

Mary, Mother of the Church, was concerned about helping others. This was seen first in her visit to Elizabeth. Even when Mary was pregnant, she left her home and journeyed to her cousin's house to help her. She cared about others first. Mary, Mother of the Church, provides an example for her children. At the wedding in Cana, Mary was also concerned about others. She was concerned about the newly-weds being embarrassed. She didn't want them to run out of wine. The Church should find an example in Mary.

Mary suffered. As Simeon said to Mary:

Behold, this child is destined for the fall and rise of many in

Israel, and to be a sign that will be contradicted (and you yourself a sword will pierce) so that the thoughts of many hearts may be revealed (Luke 2:34-35).

Mary watched as her Son was rejected and ultimately killed. The Church also suffers. But there is always the joy and hope of resurrection.

Mary's life was directed and empowered by the Holy Spirit. The Holy Spirit overshadowed her and she conceived a Son. It was also by the power of the Holy Spirit at Pentecost that the Church was born. Thus, the Church should find in its Mother an example of how to live life empowered by the Spirit.

Perhaps the most beautiful example of Mary as the Mother of the Church is found in Saint John's Gospel, when, as Jesus hangs upon the cross, he entrusts the disciple with Mary's care.

When Jesus saw his mother and the disciple there whom he loved, he said to his mother, 'Woman, behold, your son.' Then he said to the disciple, 'Behold, your mother' (John 19:26-27).

The 'beloved disciple' is symbolic of all of us, the Church. It is the 'beloved disciple' who remains while everyone else leaves Jesus to die. This is the faithful disciple and, as such, is entrusted with the care of Jesus' mother. As Church we are called to be faithful to Christ, even if it means being faithful in the face of death. We will not stand alone. Mary, Mother of the Church, was and is with us.

So Mary, as the Mother of the Church, gives us, her children, many examples of how we are to act. But what about our devotions to Mary? Is there still a place for honouring Mary?

All prayer is ultimately directed to God. Mary does not save; only Jesus does. Our prayers to Mary honour her because of the love and respect she deserves as our Mother. We do not pray to Mary in order to avoid Jesus so that we can get to God.

The Hail Mary is the best example of prayer to Mary that we have. In the second part of the prayer we say, 'Holy Mary, Mother of God, pray for us sinners...' In this prayer we ask Mary simply to pray for us. This is not uncommon since we often ask others to pray for our needs. Pray for me. Pray for my sick cousin. Pray for a friend who lost her job. Pray for us. Why not ask Mary?

A question that often arises regarding Marian devotions is about stories of the appearances of Mary: Are these to be believed or not? The love and goodness of God is revealed throughout all of creation. Thus, there is no reason why God could not choose to show further love and goodness through an apparition of Mary. Such revelations have been made popular at places like Fatima and Lourdes. There have been numerous other 'sightings' of Mary, and certainly not all of them have been officially recognised by Church authorities. It is not necessary to believe in these appearances in order to be a Catholic. Perhaps what is important about these appearances is to respect what others believe and to be grateful if these appearances lead them to faith and to God and motivate them to live according to the demands of the Gospel. As in the case of all Marian devotions, these devotions should not focus on Mary herself but, through her, lead believers to a deeper love for God.

What role does Mary have in the Church today? A very important one, for she is the Mother of the Church and serves as a loving example of how her children should know and follow Christ.

CHAPTER 23

I should pray, but how?

Roman Catholics have a two-thousand-year history of prayer, which is based upon another two thousand years of Jewish prayer and which incorporates styles from various cultures around the world. It is perhaps our diversity and variety of prayer that can sometimes overwhelm us and confuse us about prayer. There is no one correct style of prayer. However, from generation to generation, from culture to culture, particular styles have been emphasised.

This chapter will explore briefly a few of the more popular forms of prayer. Perhaps in this survey some people will be affirmed to continue their spiritual devotion, while others may be encouraged to attempt new or different forms of prayer.

Prayer is communicating with God. That is the essence of prayer. But good communication involves listening attentively as well as speaking or sending messages to another. We communicate not just with spoken words but with our bodies, in song, through dance, and through a host of other symbolic and ritual actions. Prayer brings us closer to God and God closer to us. Whatever achieves that bonding between God and us is prayer.

The greatest prayer that the Church has is the Eucharistic Liturgy, or the Mass. This is the prayer of the Church, for it draws us as close as we can humanly get to Christ. In the Eucharist we are not only drawn closer to Christ, but we are also drawn closer to each other as members of the Body of Christ. Any other form of prayer or devotion should lead us to this first prayer of the Church since the Eucharist as prayer is superior to any other prayer.

Our basic traditional prayers also form an important part of our spiritual heritage. These are prayers such as the Sign of the Cross, Our Father, Hail Mary, and Glory Be. All of these prayers are based upon the Scriptures and include the important basic elements of prayer: praying to the Triune God of Father, Son and Holy Spirit; including elements of praise and thanksgiving; and petitioning while also being open to God's will. These are prayers that children should learn almost from birth. There is perhaps no more special prayer that parents can share with their infants than to trace the Sign of the Cross on them as a sign of sharing faith with them.

Certainly among the more distinctively Catholic prayers is the rosary. While the rosary may not be as popular as it once was, it is still a widely used prayer in the Church. The rosary is clearly associated with Mary, but its origins are scriptural. The rosary began as an attempt to help the illiterate share in praying the psalms. The one-hundred-and-fifty Hail Marys correspond to the one-hundred-and-fifty psalms.

Each decade of the rosary reflects on a mystery or truth about our faith. The sorrowful, joyful and glorious mysteries are based on Scripture and our faith tradition. Today many recitations of the rosary include expanded reflections on Scripture and our faith tradition so that people can meditate upon them while saying the Hail Marys of each decade. The rosary is a powerful prayer that can be said privately or communally. It is still an important part of our spiritual life in the Catholic Church.

One beautiful memory I have of the Church from my childhood is of the dignified ceremony that accompanied the exposition of the Eucharist and Benediction. I remember the aroma of the incense and the long procession through the church and sometimes even outside the church. Exposition of the Eucharist and Benediction are still part of our spiritual lives, but the emphasis in our approach to the Eucharist has changed.

Exposition of the Eucharist and Benediction come from a time in history when people refrained from receiving Communion because they felt totally unworthy to do so. Thus, these people found grace in simply being able to gaze upon the Eucharistic Bread and to be blessed with it. This devotion provided an opportunity to come as close as possible to Christ without actually consuming the Bread.

Today we place greater emphasis on 'breaking bread' and receiving Communion. This is what Jesus commanded us to do with Eucharist when he said, 'Take and eat' (Matthew 26:26). However, exposition of the Eucharist and Benediction are still valuable forms of prayer if they draw us to the table of the Lord and do not keep us at a respectful and fearful distance.

Another form of prayer, which actually developed as a way of extending the celebration of the Mass, is the Liturgy of the Hours. This prayer was developed and used primarily by monks who would pray the psalms and proclaim the Scriptures at various times of the day and night. The Liturgy of the Hours follows the same seasonal cycle as the Eucharistic Liturgy.

Various forms of the Liturgy of the Hours have evolved for the use not only of priests and religious but also of lay people. Some parishes have recently revived this prayer, using one part of the Liturgy of the Hours – Vespers, or Evening Prayer – as a special devotion during Advent and Lent. This is a valuable way to enter prayerfully into a seasonal celebration and reflect on the Scriptures. Most Vespers services conclude with Benediction.

There are various other private and communal devotions that are still important in Catholic spirituality: devotions to Mary, to the Sacred Heart, to particular saints; Stations of the Cross; and others. While not necessarily as well attended as in the past, these devotions still serve as important ways for us to reflect on God's saving activity and love, and they can draw us closer to God. However, it is important to note again that these devotions are secondary to full participation in the Eucharistic Liturgy, which is the first and greatest prayer of the Church.

A form of prayer that has recently been revived in the Catholic tradition is charismatic prayer. This form of prayer goes back to apostolic times and focuses on praying for the gifts of the Holy Spirit. Communal charismatic prayer is often an emotional experience characterised by people raising their hands in prayer and speaking in tongues when the gift of tongues is given. Charismatics will often lay hands on individuals and pray for healing.

Not everyone feels comfortable with this ecstatic style of prayer. Yet that does not make charismatic prayer any less acceptable in the Church so long as it helps people communicate with God and leads to their full participation in the Eucharistic Liturgy.

In the past it was relatively easy to find a wide variety of Catholic prayer books that contained devotions and prayers for almost any occasion and need. While these books were helpful in providing words to pray, imagine communicating with someone you love only by reading to that person from a book. Our prayers should come from the heart, and our words should be our own personal expression of our love. When words are difficult to say, we can simply listen to what God is saying to us.

If we need words to help us pray, we needn't look far. The Scriptures provide us with some of the most beautiful prayers possible. Not only can we use the Scriptures as a prayer book, we can prayerfully enter into the Scriptures by reflecting on the meaning of a passage and opening our hearts and minds to what God might be saying to us in these words. All we need to do is read a short Gospel passage, for instance, and then put ourselves into that passage. We can imagine that we are the prodigal son, the forgiving parent, Zacchaeus, the woman at the well, the blind beggar at Jericho, and so forth. What might Jesus say to us? What would our response be to Jesus?

Some people find it helpful to keep a journal, a written record of their meditations and reflections. Journal-keeping involves us in a process that helps us write what is in our hearts. In time we can see how we have progressed in our spiritual development and perhaps even share this with someone who can guide us in our spiritual lives.

As Catholics we have a variety of ways in which we can pray. Our forms are so diverse that no one should have an excuse for not praying. Our prayers should draw us closer to God and help us live the kind of lives God wants us to live. Even if we don't feel comfortable with some forms of prayer, it is still important to respect the way others pray. It is important to remember that prayer should draw us closer to God and, thus, to each other, and that no better form of prayer can be found than our Eucharistic prayer, in which we are fully united in the Body of Christ.

CHAPTER 24

Life after death – where are we headed?

Catholic theology has shifted from emphasising an angry God who punishes sinners with eternal fire to an all-loving God who wants to welcome us back when we sin and be united with us in eternity. What has happened to hell, purgatory and limbo? Are they now regarded differently from the way they were regarded in the past?

The resurrection of the dead is central to Catholic belief. As Saint Paul says:

> But if Christ is preached as raised from the dead, how can some among you say there is no resurrection of the dead?... For if the dead are not raised, neither has Christ been raised, and if Christ has not been raised, your faith is vain; you are still in your sins (1 Corinthians 15:12, 16-17).

We believe that Jesus is risen and that he ascended into heaven. But our view of heaven has changed.

Heaven is no longer viewed as a place up in the sky where white-robed creatures gingerly float on puffy, white clouds that form a kind of celestial mist. These images may have been helpful to describe an unknown, but dwelling on them leaves a false impression of what heaven might be like.

We get some glimpses of heaven from what Jesus said. We can believe that there is plenty of room for all of us because he said, 'In my Father's house there are many dwelling places' (John 14:2). We know that our relationship with others will be different in heaven from on earth for, 'When they rise from the dead, they neither marry nor are given in marriage...' (Mark 12:25). We also know that our knowledge will be different. As Paul says, 'At present we see indistinctly, as in a mirror, but then face to face. At present I know partially; then I shall know fully...' (1 Corinthians 13:12).

What kinds of images can we then use to talk about heaven, especially in teaching children? Sometimes, with only a few words of encouragement and stimulation, things are best left to the imagination. For instance, it might be better to use abstract words that children can understand and allow them to conjure up the feelings and emotions involved. Words like happy, loving, peaceful, secure, just and beautiful, allow each person to mentally interpret what heaven might be like. Yet these words do not set an image in concrete.

These words, coincidently, describe the way things should already be going here on earth. We should make others happy; there should be peace, justice, equality, and so forth. This coincidence is no accident, for the kingdom of God is already in our midst, providing us with a preview of what is in store for us.

What kind of language can we use to describe hell? We have moved away from images of the eternal blast furnace guarded by black or green scaly creatures with horns, long tails and pitchforks in their hands. These images may have helped build the tremendous fear that motivated us to lead good lives, but all that we do should be done out of love, not fear.

Again, we can perhaps use abstract words like sadness, hatred, anger, emptiness, loneliness, selfishness, injustice, and so forth. All these work against the building of the kingdom of God and, therefore, work against what heaven can be. In other words, we begin to create our own hell on earth when we are not doing those loving acts that help build the kingdom of God.

Catholic teaching holds that hell exists. However, it is difficult to imagine how an all-loving God would allow anyone to be in hell. But God does not decide. We decide by the way we live.

If we have recently placed greater emphasis on heaven and less on hell, what have we done with purgatory? In the blinking of an eye, we can move from life to death. Yet, the next step after this life, heaven or hell, seems like an all-or-nothing proposition that just doesn't fit every situation. While probably none of us would believe ourselves bad enough to be worthy of hell, few of us would consider ourselves perfect enough to instantly be joined to God in heaven. It seems logical, therefore, that there should be some period of transition for those destined for heaven but not quite fully worthy of existing there when they die. Thus, purgatory.

Purgatory often seemed like a mini-hell. The fires were cooler, and it wasn't as scary. And there was always the knowledge that it wasn't forever.

Purgatory is not a place. It is a transition between our imperfect life and our perfect life with God. It is without time as we know it. Thus, exactly what happens in purgatory and how long it takes we do not know.

But in the transition between this life and the next, we carry not only our imperfections but also the need to make amends for the sins we have committed. Even with our sins forgiven, we must make some type of satisfaction for them. We must still 'pay a price' for the damage done by these sins. How we accomplish this is again beyond our knowledge, but it is only reasonable to assume that something must happen.

One way the Church attempted to remove the damage caused by sin was through indulgences. An indulgence is the removal of all or part of the temporal punishment due to our sins.

In the past, the Church measured indulgences in terms of days and years. However, since Vatican II, indulgences are simply stated as being partial or plenary (complete).

How do we obtain an indulgence? The Church has designated certain prayers and actions to be worthy of an indulgence and has assigned a partial or plenary value to each indulgence. We obtain an indulgence by saying the prayer or completing the action with the proper disposition and by fulfilling any other criteria the Church has established.

We can apply the indulgences we have gained to ourselves or to those who have died. We are bound with the living and the dead in the communion of saints, for all of us comprise the total Body of Christ. Just as we can pray for any living member, so can we pray for those who have died and are joined to us spiritually. Can we shorten the transition of those who are in purgatory? We can make reparation for their sins, but we cannot know how this affects their transition because there is no time in eternity.

It has been a common practice in the Catholic Church to have Masses offered for the dead. It is not necessary to 'purchase' a Mass in order to offer that Mass for someone we love. Every Mass is offered for all people, and in each Mass we have the opportunity to express our own intentions and remember the dead.

But there are other ways we can remember the dead. Our own good works can be prayers for the dead. We can donate money to a charity or organisation that was perhaps a favourite of the deceased or that exemplifies the type of life that person attempted to live. In making these donations, we can see that a person's good works live on to help others. We can offer these donations prayerfully as a way of helping the dead through their period of transition and perhaps making satisfaction for their sins. Thus, we can complete what they were perhaps unable to complete, and in the process, we help make the world a better place.

Our consideration of life after death would be incomplete without considering limbo. Limbo was viewed as a place of natural happiness without the full vision of God. While limbo was an attempt to deal with a specific situation, the Church has never made an official pronouncement concerning limbo. Today we see God's love and grace being extended to all creation. Thus, infants who die without Baptism are loved by God, and in God's love and mercy they would not be denied the opportunity of sharing in that love for all eternity.

CHAPTER 25

Is nothing sacred any more?

Today, so little seems sacred, not only in the Church but in almost every aspect of our lives. It seemed in the past that we had a more pious and reverential respect for actions and objects that we as Catholics held sacred. Look at how things have changed.

There was a time when churches were filled with statues – sometimes hundreds of them, it seemed – depicting the great women and men of our history. Now our walls are bare and clean, covered with an occasional banner celebrating a liturgical feast or season.

There was an eerie glow in Catholic churches, where people lit candles to have their prayers in the presence of the Lord all day long. Today those lights are often electric, lighted simply by flipping a switch. It's just not the same.

There was a time when people really genuflected, thumping their knees on the floor – both knees if the Eucharist was exposed. Now some modern churches don't even have kneelers.

Altar boys had to wear gloves or at least cover their hands before touching any of the sacred vessels. Today anyone touches the vessels, some of which resemble pieces found at the local arts and crafts show.

Everybody used to call a priest 'Father', and this title was always followed by his last name. Today, many are simply referred to by their first name, even if they still are addressed as 'Father'.

When my father drove past a church, he would tip his hat (men commonly wore them then), and he would say a short prayer. Today we speed by and hardly notice the buildings we pass. The Catholic churches are difficult to distinguish from the other churches, anyway.

Remember greeting the bishop and kneeling and kissing his ring?

Amazing! We never worried about catching germs from the hundreds of others who had already kissed that ring. Today we just shake hands.

I remember going camping and my mother forgetting her chapel veil. She had to wear one of my father's handkerchiefs on her head when we went to Mass.

Sundays. You could really recognise the day. People wore their 'Sunday best'. Today people wear just about anything to church and sometimes very little at that.

Sundays. Shops were closed and no one could do any 'servile work'. Today Sundays are perhaps the busiest days of the week for shoppers.

Have we lost our sense of reverence? Is nothing sacred anymore?

It seems that we have become simple and uncomplicated not only in our religious devotions and practices but in much of what we do in society. There was a time when people stood whenever the national flag passed in review. Today they sit. People used to sing the national anthem. Today they politely stand. Few even know the words.

But maybe we shouldn't be too hard on ourselves. Maybe we aren't any less respectful because we don't genuflect or kiss rings. Maybe these actions just aren't common to our experiences today. So much of our traditional religious spirit comes from a medieval European culture that reverenced its royalty. Thus, it is easy to see how the reverence shown for kings came to be applied to God, who is above any earthly ruler. Perhaps what we have today is a reserved reverence, which is simply in search of new expressions.

Our churches today are simple and functional. We are not distracted in them. Our attention is drawn to the lectern for the proclamation of the Word and to the altar for the celebration of the Eucharist. Even if our churches are not decorated with gold leaf and beautiful frescoes, we can still have a sense of the sacred if we have reverence for the Word, for Eucharist, and for all those who worship with us.

And perhaps that is the key to our understanding of the sacred today – we are moving from reverencing things to reverencing people. Jesus never gave us any directive on what we should con-

sider sacred or how we should express our reverence for God. He
simply said that if we love God, then we will love each other.

What the prophet Micah records about sacrifice could be applied as
well to reverence for sacred things. What does the Lord want from
us?

> You have been told ... what is good,
> and what the LORD requires of you:
> Only to do the right and to love goodness,
> and to walk humbly with your God (Micah 6:8).

Perhaps what we need to do today is focus on the sacredness in
people rather than on gold chalices and rings with precious jewels.

But how do we show our reverence for others? In the past, to show
our sense of the sacred, we used ritual actions. But maybe today we
can move beyond ritual acts and move to real acts – real acts of
charity, kindness and goodness.

Imagine what would happen if, instead of relying upon sacred images, we actually saw Christ in other people and we had the same
respect for people that we once had for gold vessels. What if we
guarded each person's dignity as if we really saw Christ in that person? We would usher in a new age of reverence and respect.

Imagine what the church car park would be like on Sunday morn-
ing if we had a greater sense of the sacredness of the people in the
other car. Traffic would be perpetually stopped as everyone let the
other person be first. It would be quite a change from the bumper-
to-bumper jockeying that sometimes occurs.

I remember my father's ritual for showing respect for the Eucharist
whenever he passed a church. Imagine if we had a ritual like this
one to acknowledge the presence of Christ in every shopping centre,
every office, every farm, every home we drove past. All life would
be regarded as sacred.

Is anything sacred anymore? We've made a shift in our sense of the
sacred as we have placed less emphasis on God 'out there' and
more emphasis on God 'among us.'

Maybe we need to teach our children a new reverence, a reverence
for the beauty of creation, in which we realise that we are stewards
of the earth and that God has made everything good and beautiful.

This new attitude is needed because our irreverence has caused pollution and destruction of the earth's resources.

Maybe we can teach a new reverence by showing our children how to recycle our paper, aluminium, plastic and glass. That is a lived reverence, one that is an intimate part of our lives.

Maybe we can teach our children a new sense of the sacredness of time, so that religion isn't relegated only to Sundays, so that every day becomes the Lord's day. Maybe we need to take the twenty-four hours that used to be spent exclusively as the Lord's day and spread it throughout the rest of the week. Imagine the sense of the sacred that would fill our lives if we were actively conscious of God for just two hours every day! As we begin our day, we should be able to say, 'I'm in the presence of the Lord.' When we drive to work, we should say, 'I'm in God's creation.' At work, 'These are God's people.' All time becomes God's time.

Is nothing sacred anymore? Maybe some things are not reverenced as they once were. But we should be developing a new sense of the sacred that involves not just things, but people and all the beauty of creation. If we can instill in our children a reverence for all of life, then they will have a sense of the sacred that they and their children and future generations will be able to live with.

CHAPTER 26

How is God revealed to us today?

I recently heard a beautiful story from a priest about an incident that helped him recognise the presence of God. The priest was invited to the home of a couple whose baby he was to baptise the following Sunday. As they were visiting, the baby got hungry and the mother asked the priest if he wanted to feed the baby. The priest graciously accepted the invitation. After the feeding, he dutifully put a cloth over his shoulder and proceeded to burp the baby. Soon the little infant fell contentedly asleep with its head turned toward the priest's neck.

Suddenly, the priest became aware of the baby's gentle breath on his neck – soft, rhythmic, delicate, warm. It was at that moment, as he cradled that sacred life on his shoulder, that he became aware not just of the infant's presence but of the gentle presence of God.

Sometimes God catches us off guard. Sometimes God is revealed to us in the gentle and simple ways of life.

After the prophet Elijah had slain the prophets of Jezebel, he fled in fear to Mount Horeb, the mountain of God. Elijah was directed by the Lord to stand outside of the cave where he had taken refuge, so that the Lord might pass before him and speak to him. As Elijah did so,

> A strong and heavy wind was rending the mountains and crushing rocks before the LORD – but the LORD was not in the wind. After the wind there was an earthquake – but the LORD was not in the earthquake. After the earthquake there was fire – but the LORD was not in the fire. After the fire there was a tiny whispering sound. When he heard this, Elijah hid his face.... (1 Kings 19:11-13).

For Elijah the presence of the Lord was revealed in a gentle whisper, not in the great wind, the earthquake, or the fire.

Moses had one of the most vivid personal encounters with God recorded in the Hebrew Scriptures.

> ... Moses was tending the flock of his father-in-law Jethro, the priest of Midian. Leading the flock across the desert, he came to Horeb, the mountain of God. There an angel of the LORD appeared to him in fire flaming out of a bush. As he looked on, he was surprised to see that the bush, though on fire, was not consumed. So Moses decided, 'I must go over to look at this remarkable sight, and see why the bush is not burned.'

> When the LORD saw him coming over to look at it more closely, God called out to him from the bush, 'Moses! Moses!' He answered, 'Here I am.' God said, 'Come no nearer! Remove the sandals from your feet, for the place where you stand is holy ground. I am the God of your father,' he continued, 'the God of Abraham, the God of Isaac, the God of Jacob' (Exodus 3:1-6).

Perhaps none of us will have an experience as dramatic as that of Moses encountering God in a burning bush. But maybe if we are open, we will find the signs of God's presence in the world around us. God was revealed to Moses while Moses was doing his ordinary, daily job. He was tending sheep. Perhaps in being open to the presence of God during our ordinary, daily tasks, we may find many ways in which God is revealed to us.

Perhaps we might encounter God more easily if we were less concerned with the how of revelation and more concerned with who is revealed. Who is the God we are waiting to have revealed to us?

God is the Creator. There is a beauty and order to our universe, that is beyond human understanding and comprehension. Try as we may, we find it impossible to count the stars. Scientists have attempted to give various explanations about the origins and eventual end of the universe. Yet, most of us are drawn to understand a first cause, a primal mover, whom we understand as God.

Anyone who has witnessed a birth cannot help calling the event a miracle. The human body is so carefully and intricately constructed that we cannot help asking, 'Who could have imagined and made such a magnificent creature?' The human person is a work of art designed in a way that makes the person more than just a chance happening.

The beauty of a sunrise or sunset; the gentle splashing of rain and uniqueness of a crystal snowflake; spring flowers and autumn leaves; majestic mountains and twisting canyons – all reveal a loving Creator, a God who created all things and saw that they were good. Sometimes we don't have to look too far for the revelation of God. The beauty of creation is all around us.

God is a covenant maker. God did not set the world in motion and then abandon it. God has entered into a personal relationship with people through the making of a covenant. Covenant involves the forming of a relationship. Marriage is a human example of the type of covenant relationship God established with people. In marriage two people agree to love, honour and cherish each other until death. In a covenant relationship, no matter how much we sin, how much we turn our backs on God, God never abandons us.

The focal covenant of the Hebrew Scriptures is the Sinai covenant made under the leadership of Moses. The central feature of this covenant is law, highlighted by the Decalogue, or Ten Commandments. In this covenant God promises to be the God of Israel, and the people promise to obey only the one true God. We know from history that the people did not keep their half of the agreement.

The prophet Jeremiah describes a new covenant that God will make.

> It will not be like the covenant I made with their fathers the day I took them by the hand to lead them forth from the land of Egypt; for they broke my covenant and I had to show myself their master, says the LORD. But this is the covenant which I will make with the house of Israel after those days, says the LORD. I will place my law within them, and write it upon their hearts; I will be their God, and they shall be my people (Jeremiah 31:32-33).

God is a covenant maker, one who has entered into a relationship with us and written a law in our hearts. When we act out of goodness and love, when we do what is right because of what is in our hearts, God is revealed to us.

God is a saving God. The central saving act of God for the Israelites is the Passover/Exodus event, in which the Hebrews were freed from slavery in Egypt. This dramatic event is the fore-runner of the central saving act of Jesus, who saved all people from the slavery of sin and death.

Thus, the clearest, fullest and most tangible revelation of God is found in Jesus Christ. What we see in Jesus – his compassion, love, healing touch, concern for the poor and outcast, mercy, forgiveness of sinners, mastery over sin and death – is what God is, for Jesus is God. As Jesus said, 'If you knew me, you would know my Father also' (John 8:19).

God is revealed fully to us through Jesus. How is Jesus revealed to us? Where can we find Jesus? We can encounter Christ in the word, through the reading of the Gospels as we open our hearts and minds and let the word of God penetrate our spirits. We can encounter Christ in the sacraments, especially in the Eucharist, in which we become one with Christ through the sharing of the Bread and Wine. We can encounter Christ in others – in the hungry, thirsty, foreign, poor, ill and imprisoned. 'Amen, I say to you, whatever you did for one of these least brothers of mine, you did for me' (Matthew 25:40).

Who is God and how is God revealed? God is the Creator who is revealed to us today, just as in ages past, through the beauty and goodness of creation. God, having entered into a loving covenant relationship with us, can be found whenever we respond in love. God saves us even from our deepest sins and darkest hours.

> Can a mother forget her infant,
> > be without tenderness for the child of her womb?
> Even should she forget,
> > I will never forget you (Isaiah 49:15).

God is revealed to us in a myriad of unique ways and places and at times when we may least expect such a revelation. While the fullness of revelation in time is found in Jesus Christ, God is revealed anew to each person in each age. Perhaps the best places to find the revelation of God is in our love relationships – our love for ourselves, for others, for all creation – for 'God is love, and whoever remains in love remains in God and God in him' (1 John 4:16).

CHAPTER 27

Being Catholic – what difference does it make?

When an elderly neighbour died, we went to her wake and my son asked why she didn't have a rosary in her hands. We simply stated that she wasn't a Catholic. Both of my children were surprised to learn that she wasn't a Catholic. She had been a kind, loving, friendly neighbour and a grandmother figure to my children. She never made any outward display of a specific religious belief although we sometimes talked about religion in general terms. I don't remember her ever going to church on Sunday, and there were no noticeable religious artifacts in her home. Yet, somehow, my children had grown up assuming that she was a Catholic. I wondered why they could not detect a difference, and it led me to reflect on what difference there really is in being Catholic.

There was a time not too long ago when it was easier to recognise Catholics in a crowd. Catholics went to church every Sunday and even a couple of times on weekdays for holy day Masses. They had large families, always fish on Fridays, had black marks on their heads on Ash Wednesday, and were buried with rosaries entwined in their fingers. Other than that, they looked like and usually acted like everybody else. There really didn't seem to be much of a difference between Catholics and other people.

As a child I had it drilled into my head that the Church was one, holy, catholic and apostolic. The implication was that all other Churches were not one, holy, Catholic, and apostolic.

Since Vatican II the Catholic Church has widened its vision and embrace. We can pray with those in other faith traditions. We can attend non-Catholic weddings and funerals and not fear that we are denying our Catholic faith. We have become more aware of what we hold in common with other traditions instead of emphasising what is different. We are working for unity instead of falling into divisiveness.

But some people have criticised the Catholic Church for this kind of openness and sharing, claiming that in emphasising our common inheritance we have lost sight of our uniqueness. To some, this common inheritance makes it appear that it doesn't matter what one believes just so long as one believes something. For many people, being Catholic doesn't seem to make any difference.

While it is true that we hold much in common with other Christian traditions – the Scriptures, a sacramental life, morality, spirituality, rituals, devotions and the like – there are differences. Otherwise, we would be totally united with other Christian traditions. Some of these differences are obvious while others are subtle.

The purpose of this chapter is not to elaborate on and distinguish all of the many fine points of difference between Roman Catholicism and other Christian traditions. But one way to view these differences might be to use an analogy with the flags that represent the various countries of the world. Suppose that Churches, instead of countries, have flags. Suppose that each flag represents the composite of a particular Church's religious beliefs and practices, and that the American flag represents Roman Catholicism. It is red, white and blue and has stars and stripes arranged in a unique pattern. Many other flags have red, white and blue stars and stripes, but no other flag has these arranged in exactly the same way with the same number of stars and stripes as the American flag has. The American flag, while it may have much in common with other flags, is unique.

In a similar way, as Roman Catholics, we share much with people of other religious traditions. Others may have the same 'colours' and the same 'stars and stripes', but no one else has them arranged in the same way that we, as Roman Catholics, do.

A man once came to me and wanted to know what he needed to do to return to the Catholic faith. He had been baptised Catholic and raised in a traditional Catholic family, and he had attended Catholic schools. I don't remember exactly how it had come about, but as an adult he was ordained a Lutheran minister, was married, and went with his family to Africa to serve as a missionary. Along the way he managed to obtain a degree in divinity. When he came to me, he was a doctrinal candidate in the theology department at a Catholic university.

Why did he want to return to his Catholic faith? He understood and explained in all the correct philosophical and theological jargon the differences that he had studied and had clearly outlined in his head. But from his heart he simply said that there was a difference. The difference for him came down to the sacraments, for he missed celebrating the fullness of the sacramental life in the Catholic Church. Sometimes we know that the differences are there, but they are difficult to put into words. It is mainly in our hearts that we feel them and express them.

I admire and sometimes even envy the RCIA candidates. They go through a process in which they experience something that most of us 'cradle Catholics' take for granted. The majority of them come from other Christian traditions. They are able to recognise clearly the similarities, but often they are not able to express any deep theological differences. Rather, they seem to experience the difference. For them, being Catholic often makes a difference because they feel accepted into a community that fully celebrates the life, death and resurrection of Christ and provides a vision of how to live that faith on a daily basis. They often become very alive and active in their new faith.

I remember a meeting of our parish evangelisation committee in which someone remarked that we don't need any more Catholics. What we needed, this person went on to say, were more active Catholics! For some people, being Catholic – or being anything else, for that matter – doesn't seem to make too much of a difference in their lives. But being Catholic can make a difference if we let it.

I have sometimes wondered what my life would be like if I had been baptised and raised in a Christian tradition other than Roman Catholic. I suspect that if I had been given equally good parents and teachers, and if all other things had been equal, I would probably be as involved in that tradition as I am in the Catholic tradition. But would I have sensed something missing from my life that would have attracted me to being Catholic? I'll never know.

I do know that often I have to ask myself what difference my own life makes because many times over I have willingly affirmed my Christian faith in the Roman Catholic tradition. I know that my own life can be, and I hope is, different because I immerse myself in the sacramental and scriptural life of the Catholic Church. I hope that my union with the Catholic Church positively affects the way I respond to the needs of others. I hope that my view of and respect for all of creation is different because of my lived faith as a Roman Catholic. The list could go on and on. In short, being Catholic can make a difference, if I let it make a difference – if I act on my religious beliefs.

I can study and read about the Catholic faith all I want, but it will make a difference only if I am willing to live that faith. Being a Catholic. What difference does it make? None, if I am a Catholic in name only. None, if I am a pew-sitting, Sunday-only Catholic. The difference has to come from within. The difference has to be lived every day.

The words recorded by John in the Book of Revelation and addressed to the people of Laodicea could well apply to all of us.

> I know your works; I know that you are neither cold nor hot. I wish you were either cold or hot. So, because you are lukewarm, neither hot nor cold, I will spit you out of my mouth (Revelation 3:15-16).

Being a Catholic. What difference does it make? The answer ultimately is a personal one. Each person must decide what difference religious belief makes in his or her own life. If we are not excited about our faith, if we do not live it enthusiastically every day, if we are lukewarm about it, then we will surely be spit out of God's mouth.

Saint Paul gives us this alternative:

> Let the word of Christ dwell in you richly, as in all wisdom you teach and admonish one another, singing psalms, hymns, and spiritual songs with gratitude in your hearts to God. And whatever you do, in word or in deed, do everything in the name of the Lord Jesus, giving thanks to God the Father through him (Colossians 3:16-17).

In other words, let your faith make a difference!